Public Planet Books

A series edited by Dilip Gaonkar,
Jane Kramer, Benjamin Lee, and
Michael Warner

Public Planet Books is a series designed by writers in and
outside the academy—writers working on what could be
called narratives of public culture—to explore questions
that urgently concern us all. It is an attempt to open the
scholarly discourse on contemporary public culture, both
local and international, and to illuminate that discourse
with the kinds of narrative that will challenge sophisticated readers, make them think, and especially make
them question. It is, most importantly, an experiment in
strategies of discourse, combining reportage and critical
reflection on unfolding issues and events—one, we hope,
that will provide a running narrative of our societies at this
particular fin de siècle.

Public Planet Books is part of the Public Works publica-
tion project of the Center for Transcultural Studies, which
also includes the journal *Public Culture* and the Public
Worlds book series.

Paper Tangos

public planet books

DUKE UNIVERSITY PRESS *Durham and London 1998*

Paper Tangos

Julie Taylor

Images by W. R. Dull, from a film by Fernando Solanas

Second printing, 1999

© 1998 Duke University Press

Printed in the United States

of America on acid-free paper ∞

Typeset in Bodoni Book

Library of Congress Cataloging-

in-Publication Data appear

on the last printed page of

this book.

Contents

Mi Martín, gracias.
Tu Buenos Aires, metrópoli entre
pocas, me dió a tí; y vos Martín
a la vez me diste tu Buenos Aires.

dicen que todos los Martines
se parecen hasta la muerte
pero yo sí tengo un Martín
que dice al sol detente.
—Piropo tradicional español,
siglo XIX

Acknowledgments

I have passed through many tango lessons and practices that have helped put together this vision of the tango over many years and *épocas,* but I owe the most to "lo de Carmona," of course particularly to Norma Gómez Tomasi and Ernesto Carmona, and also Marcelo Varela and Joe Rodrigo Corbata. I am particularly indebted to the analytic lucidity of Norma for her pedagogical insights that I often use in this book. Pepito de Avellaneda was my first teacher and helped me understand what I was to seek in his world.

My Argentine friends have watched me somewhat incredulously and indulgently. Rosana Guber, after innumerable drafts, finally danced. Alfredo Moreno helped me to hear the tango. Alfredo, Rosana, and Daniel Álvarez went with me to concerts we will never forget. Fernando Maresca, generous in every possible sense with his time and his space, helped ask questions and find important answers. Estela Rodríguez and I danced and thought about our

sons. La Gorda Alemán, Ester Kaufman, and Marta Jeney, and—always—Enrique Frers opened their homes to me. La familia Dickinson—Muriel and George, Charlie, Marilyn, Gabriela, as well as Roberto and John—always supported whatever I did, whether by giving me addresses in la Patagonia or finding partners for the tango, and never questioned a venture or scheme, loyalty or idea.

I remember with special clarity and warmth my conversations with women about *piropos*. All of these friends helped me in other ways and knew many other things, but their companionship and support came across in these exchanges. So my deepest thanks to Rosa María Longo de Carus, Berta Izquierdo de Villaveces, Norma Giarracca, Eugenia Beltrán, and Mónica Peralta Ramos.

All my friends and informants have remained pseudonymous in these pages.

George Marcus's and Michael Taussig's unwavering support for my work on the tango for a full decade has been key. In Houston and Buenos Aires, George, late at different nights, pointed to ways of taking this work to conclusion. The Princeton University Department of Anthropology made me welcome from 1987 to 1989, providing community and, not least, enough salary for a single mother to buy her first computer and her first fast food. Hildred Geertz and Gananath Obeyesekere in their very different ways made my time at Princeton deeply human, and Hilly accompanied me later in lonely moments with the manuscript. Dorinne Kondo read the earliest pages I had written on tango and was still there to urge me to write the last. W. R. Dull offered artistic talent and skill, reassurance, and time somehow mined out of an impossible schedule. He showed me that the project was worth finishing as we had first envisioned it, when no one else knew how to do it.

The members of my classes on experimental writing have been both supporters and inspiration for this work. In particular, Nicole Peterson, as best the group can recall, thought that some of my ideas and imagery would best be expressed in a flip book.

Fernando "Pino" Solanas and the offices of Cinesur, Buenos Aires, were always gracious, and I thank them for their permission to use the imagery from *Tangos: The Exile of Gardel.*

In the United States my greatest debt is to Santiago Villaveces Izquierdo for sharing a moment of transparent collaboration. It helped me see this as a project that belonged to all of us. It belongs to Bruce Grant, who read and read and read and responded with his usual brilliance; to Laurel George, who rendered her dancerly insights into meticulous and imaginative comments; to Erik Naumann, who helped me find music while he played the gamelan; to Deepa Reddy, whose musician's ear hears the words; and, of course, to Martín, who produced hilarious imitations of me, us, and the tango.

Choreographing a Paper Tango

When confronted with the question of illustrations for a book on dance, I realized that the real problem of this particular book on the tango was not really one of illustrations in the conventional sense. The text had sought to find words that would transmit the bodily knowledge of a dance form, knowledge that includes the reflections and associations with other experiences that the tango as genre demands. Part of that search might be shouldered by visual images, if there was a way to introduce movement onto a page of written words and to keep its presence there in such a way that readers were reminded that the words were intended to interact constantly with the image of movement to which they referred.

An obvious point of departure was film. But what was not so obvious was how to reproduce film in the pages of a book so that the central element most important to dance, the *moving* body, would appear on the pages. An initial idea of using photographs taken from a series of frames from the

film *Tango: The Exile of Gardel,* by Fernando "Pino" Solanas, became frustrating when we tried to cull sequence out of the twenty-four frames that make up a second on film. The idea of any idiosyncracy or style of movement was lost when eight photographs of contiguous film frames reproduced merely a step from one foot to the other. If, in order to depict quality of movement by involving a longer sequence, the frames chosen from the film were further apart, the movement became jerkily pixilated, or worse, the photo series became one of scarcely related poses. This last gave the very problematic impression that dance movement consists of "steps" that roughly correspond to "words," a common idea but false.

How could I obtain a danced sequence on the page that gave a notion of the quality of movement in the tango? Images, photographed from the screen projection of a film I knew by heart, covered the floor. I had cut the postage stamp–size photographs from the contact sheets that contained one out of every three or four film frames. Sometimes I got intense headaches from the visual effort as I tried to distinguish the steps performed by the infinitesimal feet of the tiny people dancing the tango. They had surprised me with their new beauty, different yet again from what I had seen on the screen aided by the step machine's frame-by-frame projection. But this was only the first new potential yielded by the search for a visual text to use with my verbal one.

Attempting to convey body knowledges not amenable to conventional rationalist analysis, I produced mock-up pages of pasted images. Some essayed detailed dissections of a tiny motion and others produced what looked like inventories of stylized positions. As I studied these with friends and students, the suggestion arose: "And if you could reproduce the movement by flipping through them?" We all laughed at the idea of a flipbook for adults, not least because we were trying to deal with a lyric and often melancholy dance—flipbooks are noted for the humor that arises from their characteristic pixilation. I cut the photographs apart again and tried to flip through the pages, stiff with paste, of minuscule images I had just put together. And precisely because we were all adults and had not seen flipbooks for some time, we all gasped at the simple magic.

But this nostalgically simple magic brought a dimension I had not expected. I watched, entranced, the lyrically fluid effect created by using photographs of one out of every four of the frames taken from the film, and then the slightly funny, jerky pixilation created by using one still out of every twelve or even every twenty. I looked for the movements that I most love in the tango, the eloquence of the woman's legs, rising and falling like breathing. But I could not find these movements because, like a breath, each occupied a fraction of a second, and so, at the most they appeared in one or two photographs. Similarly, intricate footwork, which because of problems of balance and rhythm had to be performed rapidly, disappeared into vast numbers of photographs depicting walked steps. Only an eye used to the tango could pick these gestures up and focus on them. A tiny movement captured on only one photograph would disappear in any series of numerous photos, especially when amid numerous takes necessary to depict the several steps that position the dancing couple for the statement performed by legs or feet.

A first remedy for this visual problem was to leave out some of the photos of film frames, using fewer of those that depicted preparation, so that they did not obscure resolutions or climaxes. This helped but did not completely solve the problem. I looked among the many extra photos that had been omitted in my first selection process, and restored many more of those that had been photographed from the film. The slight improvement suggested something completely new: I could add from my reserves even more photos, some of them duplicates, some of them photos of contiguous frames, contrasting with my initial use of every three or four frames of the film. The result was that the flipbook sequences could accentuate movement in a way that the original film had not, drawing attention to a movement that had moved me deeply but one that had been fleeting. What I saw corresponded to what I had seen and what I had danced in Buenos Aires. Other images not dealing with dance brought memories and associations that many Argentines make as they dance, as intimated by the fact that this imagery arises in a film about tango. This was what I had seen, what I had danced, and what many of us had felt. Insofar as those associations corresponded to what I remembered and therefore wanted to communicate about dancing, it was, as dancers sometimes say, my tango. But in this case all of it was on paper.

I was choreographing my paper tango.

A Note on Vocabulary

The tango refers to men and women, masculinity and
femininity, male and female in the context of a traditional and many-layered lore. *Tangueros* and other
Argentines often concern themselves with defining
gendered identities and roles they see as central to the
genre. I have followed their usages in these pages to describe a world in which the idea of two genders is central.
Translation from the Spanish to the English is complicated
by the problem posed by the Spanish *macho*, or male. Latin
Americans are conscious that their word has been loaded
with almost entirely negative and stereotypical meanings
outside of their cultures, something that has inevitably af-
fected its use in its original setting.

I have also used Argentine Spanish throughout,
most noticeably by adhering to the second person
singular *vos*, and its appropriate verb forms, instead of *tu*.

TO KNOW

Know, *v.*— . . . A Com. Teut. and Com. Aryan vb., now retained in Engl. alone of the Teut. languages. . . . The verb has since [1200] had a vigorous life, having also occupied with its meaning the original territory of the vb. WIT, Ger. *wissen,* and that of CAN so far as this meant to "know." Hence Eng. *know* covers the ground of Ger. *wissen, kennen,* and *erkennen,* and (in part) *können,* or Fr. *connaître* and *savoir.* . . . From the fact that *know* now covers the ground formerly occupied by several verbs, and still answers to two verbs in other Teutonic and Romantic languages, there is much difficulty in arranging its senses and uses satisfactorily. However, as the word is etymologically related to Gr., L. Fr., . . . to "know by the senses," Ger. *können* and *kennen,* Eng. *can, ken,* it appears proper to start with the uses which answer to these words, rather than with those which belonged to the archaic vb. to WIT, Ger. *wissen,* and are expressed by L. *scire* and F. *savoir,* to "know by the mind." . . .

I.1.a. trans. To perceive (a thing or person) as identical with one perceived before, or of which one has a previous notion; to recognize; to identify. . . .

II.5.a. To be acquainted with (a thing, a place, or a person); to be familiar with by experience. . . . Sometimes, to have such familiarity with [something] as gives understanding or insight.

—from the *Oxford English Dictionary*

Con este tango nació el tango y como un grito
salió del sórdido barrial buscando el cielo.
Conjuro extraño de un amor hecho cadencia
que abrió caminos sin más ley que su esperanza
mezcla de rabia, de dolor, de fé, de ausencia,
llorando en la inocencia de un ritmo juguetón.
. . .
luna en los charcos, canyengue en las caderas
y un ansia fiera en la manera de querer. . . .
Al evocarte . . .
Tango querido. . . .
Siento que tiemblan las baldosas de un *bailongo*
y oigo el rezongo de mi pasado
Hoy que no tengo . . .
Más a mi madre
Siento que llega en punta de pie para besarme
cuando tu canto nace al son de un bandoneón . . .

With this tango the tango was born and like a shout

it left the sordid mud seeking the sky.

Strange spell of love made into beat

that opened a path without any law but hope

mix of rage, pain, faith and absence,

crying in the innocence of a playful rhythm.

. . .

moon in puddles, dance of the city's edge in the hips

and a terrible yearning in love. . . .

As I evoke you . . .

Beloved tango. . . .

I feel the dance floor tremble under my feet

and I hear the plaint of my past

Today without . . .

my mother at my side

I feel her come near on tiptoe to kiss me

when your song is born in the sound of a bandoneón . . .

—from "El Choclo,"

by Enrique Santos Discépolo and

Juan Carlos Marambio Catán.

Music by Ángel Villoldo

Paper Tangos

Tango: Ethos of Melancholy

What the tango says about Argentina, the nation that created it, illuminates aspects of Argentine behavior that have long puzzled outsiders. In many foreign minds, the Argentine tourist, the Argentine military, or Argentine politicians and their followers conjure up images that, at first glance, seem to convey arrogant aggressiveness often carried to extremes that outsiders find inconceivable. What foreigners do not realize is that both public posture and private introspection constantly confront Argentines with excruciating questions about their own identity.

Answers to these questions would not seem to be forthcoming from a dance defined, as the tango is, by the world outside of Latin America. In the popular image of the tango, Valentino or a counterpart, dressed dashingly in bolero, frilled shirt, and cummerbund, flings a partner backward over the ruffled train of her flamenco costume. One or the other holds a rose. Out of this Andalucian vignette of to-

tal surrender to music and passion emerges the idea that tango lyrics express similar exuberance. Even when the words tell of lost love, treacherous fate, or an unjust world, a romantic hero supposedly sings them, gesturing flamboyantly to broadcast his sensitivity.

In dramatic contrast, in the classic Argentine tango, men with closed faces practiced the dance with each other and then, fedoras pulled down like masks, gripped women against rigid torsos sheathed in sober double-breasted jackets. Their feet, though subject to the same grim control, executed intricate figures all but independent from the rest of their bodies. Far from flamenco ruffles and roses, Argentines invented the tango at the turn of the century in the brothels on the outskirts of Buenos Aires as it thrust its slums ever further into the pampas. The dancers demonstrated their skill by performing like somber automatons, and their dance provided them with the psychic space to contemplate a bitter destiny that had driven them into themselves.

Many memories add up to a bitter and insecure melancholy that Argentines recognize as a deep current in their culture: their lack of roots in a preconquest indigenous civilization, the post–1880 wave of immigration that left three foreign-born people for every native Argentine on the streets of Buenos Aires; the continually high proportion of men to women that contributed to Buenos Aires' position as a world-renowned depot of the white slave trade; the nostalgia and resentment of newcomers when dreams of owning land became impossible to realize and other forms of success remained elusive.

So Argentines have pondered definitions of themselves for a century, initially led by the wealth of its vast plains to see Argentina as unique in South America. This left them trapped—some by painfully defensive doubt, some by arrogance—between legacies: Would Latins claim them as peers? Would Europe recognize them as Europeans? The late twentieth century has shattered this different identity for most Argentines. Yet, still they wonder. Like other Latin Americans, but perhaps even more acutely and constantly, Argentines remember that tradition had phrased their dilemma in cruel terms: Civilized or barbarian? Respected nation or banana republic? Independent agent or pawn?

The tango reflects this Argentine ambivalence. Although a major symbol of national identity, the tango's themes emphasize a painful uncertainty as to the precise nature of that identity. For Argentines, this dance is profound, although at the same time profoundly enjoyable. In the tango, they often attempt to seek out and affirm self-definition—a self-definition at whose core is doubt. The dance, sometimes involving elaborately staged behavior, can be one way of confronting this result of their search. The lyrics proclaim this doubt and reveal the intensity and depth of Argentine feelings of insecurity; they also insist that an assertive façade should betray no hint that its aggressiveness could have arisen from an anguished sense of vulnerability.

Argentines who sing, dance, or listen to the tango use it to think—hence, its intimate, reflective quality. Argentine reflection is bleak. "We are a gray nation," they say, often wistfully. Why this should be the case, making them so different from the neighboring Brazilians with their happy samba, the contrast Argentines most often evoke, they do not understand. Their literature and conversation endlessly pose the problem of identity, and they examine the tango from all angles in search of a solution. Sociologists study it, popular essayists scrutinize it, the intelligentsia listen to it in concert and debate it in lecture. Major writers such as Ernesto Sábato and Martínez Estrada have analyzed it, and Jorge Luis Borges not only studied tango themes but wrote tangos himself.

Argentines think of themselves as reluctant to give in to exuberant emotion, much less to its display. Proudly in control, yet sometimes, for precisely this reason, trapped in themselves, Argentines channel their characteristic combination of inhibitions and introspection into a particular form of brooding that amounts to a national institution: *el mufarse*. The mood relates closely to the tango. Mufarse involves bitter introspection, but Argentines add to this emotion a clear sense of self-indulgence when they give in to a *mufa*. It is a depression, but with a cynicism about the depression itself, an awareness that it can feel good to throw practicalities aside, have a *vino tinto* or one of the demitasse coffees over which many a tango was written, and contemplate one's bad luck and its universal implications.

Tango fans in particular traditionally passed time constructing complex personal philosophies of life, suffering, and love—philosophies that surprise outsiders who do not expect such elaborate abstractions as common themes of popular culture. The tango postulated both a worldview and a special person who held it in its purest form, the *tanguero.* This classic lore underlies all subsequent understandings of the tango. In the classical version, a man discusses philosophy or sings tangos about it with the understanding that he is an essentially sensitive and vulnerable being in a life that forces him to cover up these qualities with the façade of the experienced, polished, suave, and clever man of the world. This tanguero is idealistic, but he is not *gil*—the *lunfardo,* or argot, for the stupidly innocent. He tries to avoid revealing the naïvete inherent in the male sex, but *el qué dirán,* the what-they-will-say, obsesses him and he sees the rest of the world as mocking observers. He devotes himself to constructing a front that will obviate a smothered laugh or a wink behind his back. By contrast, the gil foolishly acts upon ideas that, if he had learned anything at all from experience, should have been destroyed long ago and relegated to their place as useless though forever-cherished childhood dreams.

The city and the women who live there most often waken the man of the tango from his dreams to the real nature of the world. Women of the tango were themselves betrayed by the promise of better life in the city, and they often long to return to the

innocent cotton dresses they had worn in the barrio of their past. But many such women could reach for material success and fame only in the cabaret, a world from which there is no turning back to decent society. The city center represents wealth, success, fame—a chance to climb the social ladder at the price of the human values left behind. But the emptiness of these goals provokes the tango's lament for the lost neighborhood or barrio on the edge of Buenos Aires, where the sophisticated but disillusioned tango singer spent his youth.

Through the first decades of the twentieth century, construction was the city's major industry. Time after time the burgeoning city center obliterated its old limits. Asphalt and concrete covered the barrios, the neighborhoods that were half city and half country, where local soccer teams played in empty fields on weekend afternoons while, under grape arbors, families passed around gourds of *mate* prepared with fresh *cedrón* leaves, and sweethearts arranged to meet in the evenings in entryways beneath the streetlamps. Tangos often sing of the man who comes back to his barrio with the hope that it might have escaped change.

Most of all, such a man returns to search for his mother and the values he deserted along with her when he was seduced by the city and its women. Ironically, the mother to whom entire tangos sing homage is in fact the first of the women to betray a man, by her very insistence on ideals that can never apply to reality outside her tiny home in the remembered barrio. So many tangos sing of betrayal by a woman that, according to the Argentines themselves, other Latin Americans call the tango "the lament of the cuckold." Man, the idealistic, dreaming innocent, is deceived and thus initiated in the ways of the world by Woman, the wily, unfeeling, vastly experienced traitor.

Inevitably, men put their faith in these sophisticated women, who became independent, powerful, and calculating creatures out for their own selfish ends. Inevitably, these beautiful but deadly women abandon the men they choose to exploit and move on to others who offer greater wealth and shallower spirits. The victims of the female sex find themselves helpless, destitute, and alone with no recourse but to sing the tangos that muse on their downfall.

> . . . si un día por mi culpa
> una lágrima vertiste
> porque tanto me quisiste
> sé que me perdonarás.
> Sé que mucho me has querido,
> tanto, tanto como yo.
> Pero en cambio yo he sufrido
> mucho, mucho más que vos.
> No sé por qué te perdí,
> tampoco sé cuándo fué
> pero a tu lado dejé
> toda mi vida.
> Y hoy que estás lejos de mí
> y has conseguido olvidar,

soy un pasaje de tu vida,
nada más.

. . . if one day it ever was my fault
that you shed a tear
because you loved me so
I know you will pardon me.
I know you have loved me deeply,
as much as I have you.
But I by contrast have suffered
much, much more than you.
I don't know why I lost you,
nor do I know when it was
but I left all my life
at your side.
And today, now that you are far away
and have managed to forget,
I am just a passage in your life,
nothing more.
—from "Toda mi vida," by José María Contursi.
Music by Aníbal Troilo

8

The only man who could resist city women and hold on to barrio values while conquering the sophistication of Buenos Aires and other world capitals was Carlos Gardel, whom Argentines unanimously praise as the greatest tango singer of all time. Carlitos was killed in a plane crash in 1935, but his features are still as familiar as the Argentine national colors, which often surround the face that smiles down on passengers from decals in taxis and buses. That face was one of Gardel's greatest achievements. The illegitimate son of an immigrant washer-woman had taken care to leave no trace of his humble background or foreign origins in the calculated combination of dazzling smile, tilted hat, and impeccably arranged tuxedo. He incarnated the ideal of the Argentine as quintessentially urban. But he never allowed his urbane elegance to undermine his values or his loyalties. The myths of Carlos Gardel further relate that from the pinnacle of his success in the city center, he remembered the neighborhood friends of his youth, and that he longed for Argentina while he triumphed in European capitals. Even more important, he resisted the glamour of the women surrounding him and remained faithful to his mother: Gardel never married, and his mother's tomb adjoins his. Carlitos took the tango as song to its apogee, yet he restates more than an aesthetic ideal each time an Argentine listens to his recorded voice and pronounces the familiar saying, "He sings better every year."

As both artist and man, Gardel commands special concentration on his rendering of tango lyrics. But tango enthusiasts pay careful attention to other singers' renditions as well, even though the lines are often already so well known that all Argentines quote them as proverbs relevant to daily situations. A traditional rule, no longer always followed or even known, dictates that Argentines not dance to a tango that is sung. Tangueros believed that while dancing they could

not attend properly to the music and lyrics, or hear their own experience and identity revealed in the singer's and musicians' rendering of profoundly Argentine emotions. The singer of the tango shares his personal encounter with experiences common to all Argentines. He does not need bold pronouncement or flamboyant gesture; his audience knows what he means and his feelings are familiar ones. They listen for the nuances, emotional and philosophical subtleties that will tell them something new about their guarded interior worlds.

When they dance to tangos, Argentines traditionally contemplate themes akin to those of tango lyrics, evoking emotions that, despite an apparently contradictory choreography, are the same as those behind the songs. The choreography also reflects the world of the lyrics, but indirectly. The dance portrays an encounter between the powerful and completely dominant male and the passive, docile, completely submissive female. The passive woman and the rigidly controlled but physically aggressive man contrast poignantly with the roles of the sexes depicted in the tango lyrics. This contrast between two statements of relations between the sexes aptly mirrors the insecurities of life and identity.

An Argentine philosophy of bitterness, resentment, and pessimism traditionally has had the same goal as a danced statement of machismo, confidence, and sexual optimism. The traditional tanguero's schemes demonstrate that he is a man of the world—that he is neither stupid nor naive. In the dance, the dancer acts as though he has none of the fears he cannot show—again, proving that he is not gil. He refers to an experience of total control over the woman, the situation, the world—an experience that can allow him to vent his resentment and express his bitterness against a destiny that denied him this control. The tango can also give dancers a moment behind the protection of this façade to ponder the history and the land that have formed them, the hopes they have treasured and lost. Ernesto Sábato echoes widespread feeling in Argentina when he says, "Only a gringo would make a clown of himself by taking advantage of a tango for a chat or amusement" (1963: 16).

While thus dancing a statement of invulnerability, the somber tanguero sees himself—because of his sensitivity, his great capacity to love, and his fidelity to the true ideals of his childhood years—as basically vulnerable. As he protects himself with a façade of steps that demonstrates perfect control, he contemplates his absolute lack of control in the face of history and destiny. The nature of the world has doomed him to disillusionment, to a solitary existence in the face of the impossibility of perfect love and the intimacy it implies. If by chance the woman with whom he dances feels the same sadness, remembering similar disillusion, the partners do not dance sharing the sentiment. They dance together to relive their disillusion alone. Many years back, in one of the most traditional of Buenos Aires dance halls, a young man turned to me from the fiancée he had just re-

linquished to her chaperoning mother and explained, "In the tango, together with the girl—and it does not matter who she is—a man remembers the bitter moments of his life, and he, she, and all who are dancing contemplate a universal emotion. I do not like the woman to talk to me while I dance tango. And if she speaks I do not answer. Only when she says to me, 'Omar, I am speaking,' I answer, 'and I, I am dancing.'"

Double Lives

T here have been times in Buenos Aires when I knew that at any moment I wanted to dance, I could take a bus to some place in the city where people would be dancing the tango. They, like me, danced for the pleasure of it. But for me as a woman and for my woman friends in the growing tango underworld in Buenos Aires, the tango rewarded and frustrated us. In all eyes, women have the most difficulty laying claim to a dance that they love and that they see as beautiful. Both men and women, inside and outside of the dance halls, tell me that in their eyes, the tango dances around relations between men and women, relations that dancers and observers alike question. And many Argentine dancers and observers imply that, especially in the wake of decades of political violence, they also feel the tango bears the weight of other forms of authoritarianism.

My rounds of classes, where *profesores* teach tango steps and postures, *prácticas* or practice sessions, where aficionados work on steps together,

and the *milongas,* or dances, were more exotic to most denizens of the same city than to foreigners who often expect strange things of my life in a city strange to them. *Porteños,* Argentines of the port capital of Buenos Aires, outside the relatively small world of the dance halls, know the tango to be vaguely related to a particular Argentine destiny. But they are astounded to know that the classes, practices, and milongas are going on all over Buenos Aires. They are astonished to think that people like me and people like themselves just walk in, right off the street, to these unlikely places and begin to dance. They are incredulous when they try to imagine that I know many of their compatriots for whom, like me, it is normal to go about ordinary business in the city of over ten million inhabitants, with a pair of extra shoes just in case the opportunity to dance presents itself.

Many Argentines are bemused or embarrassed when foreigners expect them to be able to tango. For some, the tango's danced statements of power relations, especially between male and female dancers, alienate them completely. I have taken friends to practices where we both discovered that they had never seen the tango danced off stage. They were surprised at the discovery and shocked at what they saw. Others began classes but found them impossible to continue: "I had to stop when the profesor told me, 'Rosa Lucía, you must become nothing more than the shadow of Daniel.'" Still other acquaintances dance but feel negatively about the inequalities they feel they are performing; they find as well that men and women disagree about how to interpret those asymmetries. Performers and aficionados, even if only tentatively, rework the tango's content and choreography. But the limits of this process are continually under discussion. Men and women do have to dance together. They modify the dance where change is possible, yet change in itself is a subject of heated debate. "But suddenly this may no longer be tango," a profesor thought aloud one evening. "And the tango is what we have."

Like most of the Argentines dancing the tango in Buenos Aires, I worked at something else and danced in my extra time because I loved it. I worked in Argentina as a researcher and university professor. I had begun my university studies halfheartedly, with the idea of returning as soon as possible to a life as a ballet dancer. Instructors in my required social-science distribution courses at Harvard suggested that I might have the talent to construct an academic career in anthropology, of which I had never heard. This, they pointed out, could last me somewhat longer than the usual retirement age of well below thirty in classical dance. To prove their point, they sent me off to study ritual dance on the coast of Perú. Afraid that I might never be able to return to a continent that enchanted me, I traveled from Cartagena to Tierra del Fuego by land and fell in love with Buenos Aires on the way. I arranged all my further studies around returns to Argentina, paying little attention to the incomprehensible letters from my friends, who could not understand

that I was missing landmark dates and people in their lives.

My first research project in the country focused on the tango and its importance to Argentines, a natural subject for a ballet dancer turned anthropologist. But, as Argentina passed through the excruciating years of worsening dictatorships, and became ever more clearly plagued with terrible problems, I shifted my focus to research on subjects that seemed more pressing than picturesque.

I had returned to Buenos Aires on the night of a military coup. All of us watched as the political situation unraveled, finally entering a state of permanent crisis. Many of my Argentine friends were also researchers: We felt transfixed, caught in the blinding searchlights of impending doom. We turned our attention and professional talents to attempts at understanding the processes that swept us up for two decades—and have yet to let us go. One of those decades witnessed the savage 1976–1983 *Proceso*, the dictatorship of the Junta that added the word *desaparecido* to the world's vocabulary.

Participating in the dance had not been a formal part of my early research. I was too young to know how to wrench around my academic discipline to include it. Beyond that, I carried out this initial work at a time when middle class porteños made a point of listening to tango but never dancing it. They also made the point that their city had invented the tango and only they could appreciate its spirit. But on my travels, I found that everywhere throughout the nation others claimed the tango as their heritage as Argentines. I had long talks with aficionados in the far North; I learned steps in the central pampas; and I began to dance on an Argentine ship out of Tierra del Fuego heading toward the Argentine Antarctic.

The Argentines who started my long apprenticeship in the tango were the young people of the typical pampa town of Pehuajó, who celebrated spring's arrival in September with a combination of car races and dances that mixed the cumbia and the tango night after night. The mother of the family with whom I was staying also helped with her comments each morning about the dance the night before. She would come to the room I shared with her daughter, bearing the necessary hot water, dry *yerba,* and sugar for the preparation of the mate gourd she'd hand us to wake us up. In homes in Pehuajó, hilariously laughing Argentines watched me stumble through my first milonga, a word that refers not only to occasions when the tango is danced but also to the breathlessly fast dance itself, to all my intents and purposes of that time, a rapid form of the tango. Exhilarating and exhilaratingly lovely, influenced in different forms by country dances and the African-Argentine rhythms that also inform the tango itself, the milonga is seldom seen outside Argentina.

But over the following years, I seldom danced again. During those years much had happened to all of us. The terror of the dictatorship's Dirty War against its opposition, and anything that remotely resembled an opposition, was so intense that, to

this day, many of us automatically look around, frightened, when certain subjects come up in conversation. We tried to push our lives ahead but could only limp forward as we looked for missing pieces: friends who had disappeared, others who were forced into exile by fear and physical danger, and still others who had shifted residence several times. Friendly meetings that had occurred regularly became erratic or nonexistent. In 1979—the year of the most intense terror—my son was born in Buenos Aires. His father was a Patagonian who, like many Patagonians, was Chilean by nationality and Argentine by upbringing. I thought initially that I had lost the connections of my social life because of the unending work of caring for a newborn; only much later did I realize how many people shared the same weight of total isolation. So I avoided bombs on the way to the pediatrician and tried to resist the urge to snatch the baby and run when the police cordoned off our block because of explosives in a building they wouldn't identify. And I wondered why I had so few people to call for advice on how to deal with an infant.

In the effervescent release from fear at the fall of the Junta, we timidly began to recreate our social worlds and to compare notes. The exiles into which Argentines had been thrust became familiar episodes—internal exile, as it was known, as well as external. We had been engaged in the lonely task of inventing Argentine culture on our own, often far from Argentina, investing memories and customs with the meaning we each pulled out of our pasts. Nostalgic as we

were, many bits and pieces of everyday life had been permeated with longing for a lost peace: food, trivial news and
gossip, and the tango.

The tango's meanings shifted not only to include a unique
Argentine identity, but also to express as well the particular
forms of disorientation, loss, and uncertainty of the nation's
fate inculcated by years of terror. This was the first deep
relationship that I felt between violence and the tango. In
the initial optimism of the return to democracy, I had given
no thought to how the remnants of that relationship with fear
might cling to a dance form. Yet it was, after all, surviving in
a society still ridden with fear.

On one of the city's sunny but cold July winter days, I
found myself alone in downtown Buenos Aires. My son was
away on a visit. I was between tasks. My bags were all
packed, as I had moved out of one apartment but was unable
to move into the next. Startled, I realized that I was free to
look for the addresses that, for years, I had jotted down one
by one, never really believing I would someday be able to
follow them out—to people who taught the tango and to
places where it was danced. I pulled innumerable scraps of
paper from notebooks, pockets, and handbags and began by
making my way through miles of ramshackle corridors to find a tiny set of offices whose bemused inhabitants gave me mimeographed sheets of addresses of neighborhood cultural programs that
included tango. The night of that same day, in my
first class, other students and onlookers praised

and criticized teachers and dancers, providing information that sent me on more journeys all over the city, piecing together a universe I had not known existed. The rhythm of my classes and practices rapidly accelerated.

"But *why* do you do all this dancing?" an acquaintance asked in a conversation with several unbelieving Argentines. Another member of the group, who had initially expressed similar bewilderment, suddenly lit up. She announced to the rest of the group in the Italian understood on porteño streets, "Perché le piace!" Because she likes it. And she was right. I was in a world deeply familiar from my years as a dancer, a world that gave me back my body and the modes of learning with it and from it that had formed my earliest perceptions. As the tango threw all this sharply into focus, I recuperated something that had been obliterated by years of rational argument. I recuperated ways of knowing, ways of knowing art, ways of knowing violence, ways of knowing fear—ways of knowing them to be bound up together in a body to which I could lay a tentative claim.

The feeling of reconnection and restoration was overwhelming enough to outweigh the very real fear that I felt at confronting this particular dance, long before I discovered that I was not the only person to feel it. The fear was not less deep and vivid because I acted in spite of it. I thought it had only to do with my own life history, and as I turned it over in my mind, I never linked it with other dancers or with the terror from which we all had just emerged. It had to do with the feeling of returning to class, where someone would grant approval or mete out punishment. The people in my life who had done this had been men, and here I was, seriously considering not only putting myself into the position of being judged by a teacher, but literally putting myself into the hands of men who would all be in a position to criticize me. I remember walking down the street to my first class and thinking how difficult this kind of situation had been in my life. How could I solicit it again? And then I thought of what I would lose if I gave in to the painful memories. I took a deep breath and walked through the door into a group of people who, unbeknownst to me and to greater or lesser degrees, were similarly fearful. Somewhere in my mind I saw this second link between tango and violence as I began again to dance.

Suddenly, we were staring at each other in disbelief as the call was issued for an act of presence in the central Plaza de Mayo to celebrate twenty years since the *golpe militar*, the Junta's coup. The terror had ended with the trial and punishment of the Junta, but soon thereafter the Law of Due Obedience had left us with the constant doubt as to whether a strange face might be that of an assassin or torturer. Later came the Presidential Pardon of the Junta itself. Crime, major and minor, ran rampant, apparently with total impunity. Still later, the tragic bombing of the Jewish Community Center, the 110-year-old AMIA, with 245 casualties, echoed painfully with events and emotions under the Junta: terror, guilt, grief. Over all this time, I had found to my surprise that

some of the weight of past terror was borne by the tango.

I expected these links to grow weaker with time. The intensity of the pleasure of dancing, I thought, would replace them. And if not, the associations with terror would diminish the pleasure, and I would no doubt find it unbearable to dance. Neither occurred. The pleasure deepened; the fear continued to surface; and I found dancing the paradox irresistible.

Search Milonga

Most of the places I have gone to dance lead a double life. I manage to describe the locale and suddenly, with an exclamation, the person listening to me recognizes it as the seat of a soccer club or the scene of a wedding or a bachelor farewell, or as a nightclub or cafe. I took an Argentine friend who had never seen the tango danced in her life to a practice in the place she realized—after some perplexed musing—was precisely where her father- and mother-in-law had celebrated their golden wedding anniversary. Another friend realized one year that I danced in the studios built as appendages somewhere between permanence and total precariousness on the *azotea*, the flat roof above her father's union hall, the Center for Retired Grocerymen. The retired grocerymen and others were always dancing below us: flamenco, folklore, cumbia, and, every Thursday, tango. At a session that failed, probably because of being on the edge of a barrio with a reputation for being tough, we never got to dance in the tiny hall of the Ex–Maritime Machinists, with its glowing wooden floors under elaborate moldings and a chandelier.

I danced a whole season in a museum. In off hours, the profesor, a permanent guard, would lead me through new steps to the music of a boom box surrounded by priceless pieces of art. Many of us, initially aghast, gradually forgot that this was not the most natural place in the world to perform. The tango and its students who came and went every day were somehow invisible. A dance hall lodged between a striptease joint and a porn movie theater in the very center of town forced me to look carefully left and right before dashing in the door, to avoid possible detection by anyone I knew. The dance hall was converted each night into a tawdry cabaret as the tango dancers moved from their late afternoon classes to the practice sessions of the early evening elsewhere and, possibly, to a milonga still later on. I had found these classes thanks to a Swiss tango enthusiast who, standing on a street corner after class late one night, offered to recommend some of his favorites and brought up the cabaret address on his hand-held computer in response to the command "Search Milonga."

I had neglected to stop by one of my now favorite locales for a year because I had heard upon arriving anew in Buenos Aires that it had been condemned by the municipality. If it was a condemned building, I reasoned, it could not be a dance hall. But at practice one night, some students who had

seen me lecture at the National University—where there are enough tango dancers to generate reports of disbelief that the person they are used to seeing in dance halls is also an academic—hailed me and asked if I wanted to go to the milonga with them at the very place I had thought was closed. When I asked, they responded somewhat cryptically, "Of course it's closed, but there is still dancing—igual se baila." My friends had already gone by the time I left practice; so I decided to walk the few blocks to the milonga by myself, trying to recall exactly where it was. When I thought I should have arrived, I could see no sign and no one else on the midnight street. Perplexed, I was wondering how a condemned building might look, when a couple emerged from a door indistinguishable from others. As they walked away, the two called over their shoulders that if I was looking for the milonga, that was it. I crossed the street, pushed open the door, and walked in.

The condemned building was dark, but tango music boomed through its spaces. I located a woman who seemed to be in charge and asked how to pay. In general, one pays upon leaving practices and classes, but upon entering milongas. To my surprise, I learned that we were to pay whatever we would or could upon leaving. Still puzzled, I took the candle handed to me and made my way toward an interior area. There were no professional dancers present that I could identify peering through the gloom. But the couples on the floor were good. Their performance was enhanced by the fact that the wall behind them, if partly crumbling, was painted with swathed theatrical curtains. The rest of us, when not dancing, sat at tables, to which we stuck our lighted candles in their own melted wax, and drank wine that we ordered from figures that appeared and disappeared in the night.

I was completely absorbed in the shadowy beauty of the atmosphere and the dance. Loud raps sounded on the door, and we exchanged looks. None of us had knocked upon entering. It was the police. We could hear voices rising and falling. Some of the dancing couples did not even stop. Others, in conversations at the tables, hesitated and then went on. But tension, fueled by memories of the terror of the recent dictatorship, permeated the dark ambience. I had been warned many times about drugs and the tango, and I wondered if this was the first indication of drugs that I had encountered. Or was it only that a condemned building could not also be a dance hall? In the dark, someone approached the outer door and reported back that those in the outer room were explaining to the police that this was a private house and a private party and that without a warrant, no search could be carried out. Inside, we assumed that this logic would be unlikely to hold back aggressive *cana* or cops; but the music continued and the dancers did not stop.

Suddenly the police were gone, leaving a wake of such intense relief that many dancers dispersed into the dawn still uncertain what had happened but unwilling to stay to find out, ridden with memories of persecution. I caught up with a friend at a bus stop where we decided, instead, to share a cab. He had been dancing, he said, and could see something of what occurred each time he passed the outer door. The last he had seen before the police surprisingly abandoned the premises was the young man who had claimed he was hosting a private party stripping down to his underwear as proof of his loud claims that at his own party he could do anything he wanted.

Cobblestone

Upon entering a practice or a class from the street, particularly in the wintery Junes and Julys of my usual visits, prospective dancers must first unbutton, unzip, and unwind their protections against the porteño night outside. It is useful to keep track of the heating in the different dance halls in order to arrange layers of clothing such that a final layer will still be decent after the first minutes of warming up. Women at this point sit in chairs around the edge of the dance floor and attend to their footwear. Some produce a pair of old shoes; others slip handsewn elastic loops, *elastiquitos,* around the instep of street shoes. Every year, more and more bring out a pair of special shoes. These special shoes, unlike ballroom dancers' shoes used in the Northern Hemisphere, have normal leather soles, not suede. Those whose day's activities have not allowed them to arrive dressed to dance retire to a bathroom to put on elasticized jeans or to strip off trousers to reveal leggings underneath.

Those who remain seated, both men and women, chat about dance steps and styles or scrutinize those performing on the floor. Gossip around the dance floor distinguishes dancers by skill, but most importantly by style. Argentines claim they can always spot foreigners, no matter how proficient, because they "lack cobblestone," the embodiment of the quality that only the urban streets of Buenos Aires can impart: *adoquín.* But Argentines, too, are distinguishable one from the other. Many Argentines, of course, are rank beginners. Others display different degrees of cobblestone. And onlookers identify the different styles with the *academia* or *salón,* often related to class, in contrast with the *tango milonguero,* an older form believed to be inherited directly from tangos as danced in the courtyards or patios of brothels and slums that are now memories.

Older tangueros and the very young who seek either a personal trademark or an authentic tango, without quite knowing what that is, are more likely to adopt the milonguero style. Some are quite proselytical about the tango milonguero, urging other couples to assume the characteristic posture that transforms all steps. The woman moves her hand from her partner's shoulder up around almost to the other shoulder, holding his neck in the crook of her arm, her face joined to his. Tango steps performed in this position demand that the lower bodies separate, with the frequent effect that the woman dancer appears to be almost diagonally supported on the man who remains upright. Only once in the

long debate about milonguero style did I hear a technical description: Instead of hitting the beat exactly, dancers perform embellishments until the last possible instant, when they actually shift weight. Whether or not milonguero style is authentic tango, whether or not it allows steps to be correctly performed or performed at all, whether or not the woman's waist should "break"—if so, how far, and if not, how to avoid it—are all subjects of great interest. The milonguero position and its play with the feet are options at any moment in any tango for any tanguero.

A Musical Landscape

An Argentine tango announces itself by its inescapable rhythm. Once, I heard a recording of a selection of tangos by a favorite orchestra. But each time I listened to it anew, I grew increasingly aware of something gnawing away at my enjoyment. I began to pay attention in order to pinpoint it. Finally I figured out which tango jarred my ear and looked it up: it was the world famous "Jalousie," clearly a "European" tango—composed by a Dane and lacking the stylistically emphatic beat of the Argentine tango. In shabby corridors, up dark stale stairways, through neighborhood doorways, the first sounds of a class or practice are those of the definite and comfortingly heavy beat. Closer to the dancers and their music, plaintive dissonances make their statements of the tango's melancholy themes. Melody frequently stays in the background. Like tango lyrics, melodies are so well known that listeners take them for granted and remain intent on sorting out the arrangements.

By traditional rule—strict ten years ago but not always followed or even known today—tangueros do not dance to tangos that are sung. Lyrics are meant for listening, not dancing, which in turn demands silence. Tangos can be interpreted in styles that are not consistently sad; in particular, early *Guardia Vieja*, or Old Guard, tangos come from an era "when the tango was happy," as the worn cover of one of my favorite albums states, by the Cuarteto Polenta, a title that might best be translated as the Gumption Quartet. And, city milongas and the *milongón* are related to African-Argentine beats, virtually always intensely gleeful, in contrast to the haunting country *sureras* or pampa milongas, milongas that are seldom danced. Yet the tango makes sad harmonies that render its inexorable beat a tragic statement.

When best played, its main instrument, the *bandoneón,* a German invention originally intended to be a portable organ for hymns, "weeps" in the hands of a lionized musician.

> El duende de tu son, che bandoneón,
> se apiada del dolor de los demás
> y al estrujar tu fueye dormilón
> se arrima al corazón que sufre más.
>
> The soul of your sound, che bandoneón,
> Takes pity on the sadness of others

and, wringing your sleepy bellows
comes close to the heart that suffers most.
—from "Che Bandoneón," by Homero Manzi.
Music by Aníbal Troilo

Other instruments sob in gifted performance: the bandoneón of Aníbal Troilo, beloved as "Pichuco," or Astor Piazzolla's bandoneón along with Antonio Agri's violin; the saxophone of Julian Vat or of Miguel de Caro. Once, in a cafe sometime around two in the morning, the bass player from the orchestra at the opera house, the Teatro Colón, still in tuxedo, climbed on stage with a bandoneonista from the audience and the two sounds cried for hours together. In a practice where the profesor prided himself on his careful choice of music and his effort at finding lost performances, the plaintive, plaintive sounds made by the folklorist Hugo Díaz on the harmonica felt like blows to the solar plexus.

Escrachando: Members of the Cast

If they are in a class, dancers wait for the profesor to assign them a partner, or each can agree with a fellow member of the class to try to smooth out a difficult step. If the session is a practice, participants know each other by sight, so they are likely to greet each other cordially and proceed to dance.

A predictably large number of aspiring professionals looks on: would-be performers and teachers, as well as the occasional dancer who has made it onto the stage and has come back to practice and to greet friends. Only one of the young successes is thought *never* to return to practices or even milongas except to attract attention to himself. For this he is duly censured in the world he left behind. Sometimes ancient and revered dancers sit surveying the assembly, unable to dance but still willing to give opinions and tips to experienced dancers. The gossip includes projected shows, tryouts, new choreography, the inauguration of studios, memories of past tours and hopes of new ones. Those who consider themselves professional instructors pose a problem in the practices. They would never appear in a class held by another profesor. But although each practice is held by a profesor with the prime purpose of allowing his or her own students to practice, other potential profesores hustle for students, surreptitiously handing out their cards after each set.

In the classes and even at some of the milongas, there is a group made up of psychotherapists, some avoiding each other and their professional identity while others proffer interpretations of the different teachers, dancers, and sometimes of the dance itself. Their diagnoses are refuted or tried on for size by anyone who happens to hear them, professional dancers and students, aficionados and dilettantes. Once, I naïvely ventured to defend the tango from accusations of exaggerated machismo by suggesting that the presence of such a highly educated group indicated a dilution of traditional values linked with masculinity. The Argentines in

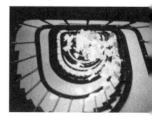

the conversation managed an impossible combination of sneer and hearty laughter, advising me that, in their experience as part of the population with the highest number of psychiatrists per capita in the world, this was no guarantee.

Franklin, friend of all the women, who spoke from his authority as a fine dancer and older male, could confront the psychiatrists and even the profesor when he cared to do so. Franklin was a favorite personage at classes, practices, and milongas, where he was sure of his own style and nonjudgmental with his partners. My interactions with him caused a great deal of hilarity: "Why is this name the only word you can't pronounce?" people would laugh incredulously. "You need to say 'FRAHNkleen,' 'FRAHN-kleen.'" I would be reproached every time I lapsed into something resembling the name of a North American president. Franklin was a union organizer who had risen to his rank from the kind of childhood to which many tangos allude. He had a wonderful car, and he would transport some of us from class to practice or to a club or milonga while he regaled us with tales of learning the tango at the barrio soccer clubs to which he had graduated after learning *futbol* in the plazas, with a ball made by winding rags around one another. Franklin had a tragic mystery in his personal life that had compelled him to dance every night; so it was only a matter of searching several different tango gatherings every night until we would catch up with him. We often wanted to consult him about style or steps, or sometimes on how to deal with the male profesores whose attitudes toward the tango and toward their students Franklin could translate because many of them had emerged from a past like his. He could poke fun at the stylized elegance of *tango de academia* as the only student the profesores would respect. And sometimes we just wanted to hear the news of his latest labor slowdown or listen for clues to the melancholy that emerged from his stalwart cheerfulness from time to time.

Classes often bring together such intense people—both dancers who aim for a career in teaching or on the stage, and others attracted by this environment. Practices, by contrast, attract these people and also large numbers of participants who take the tango less seriously and for whom, therefore, it has become integrated into everyday life. The late 1980s tango boom in the Northern Hemisphere continues to reverberate in Argentina—not only are there more Argentines who dance for the love of it, but also there are more foreigners who come to learn to teach. All types mix in the practices.

At practices, the very young businessman was a stylish dancer, despite having left dancing for several years while he studied martial arts. His was almost purely a *tango de salon*, but because it so suited his unusually tall and spare figure, observers forgot to comment. The soccer player had taken up the tango upon his return to Argentina, after his stint as a professional *futbolista* in Europe. Now back home, he worked as a coach and had started up a business manufacturing fire extinguishers. But, he clarified, he always

had his soccer clothes and his ball in the trunk of the car, "ready to play." At night, he danced the tango with the grace of a natural athlete, and a natural at the national sport, at that. That put him, too, above comment. But the very blond, slight Argentine, who always appeared in a three-piece suit that draped rather than fitted, and who danced wonderfully, was admired for displaying, if not new steps, the far more important perfect "cobblestone." Then there was the dancer who appeared consistently, year after year, in the different practices I managed to find. We knew him as Ricardo Jol, a name whose sounds fit a Latin identity well enough. But once, while I was talking to an older, fourth-generation Anglo-Argentine couple about their friends the Hall family, I could not help but mention the coincidence. "Oh no!" they gasped. "Not Richard Hall! Dancing the tango? Do you suppose his parents know?" Ricardo must have been over forty; his cobblestone was nearing perfection.

Many women shared my background in classical ballet. Their presence reassured me in its familiarity. Often dressed in black, often with a leotard or tights as at least one element of their dress, they would sit at the edge of the class, resting against one another, arranging one another's hair. If the classroom is a recycled dance studio, their reflections in the mirrors double their groupings. One hot January, we waited on the terrace outside a class still in progress, whose music we could hear clearly through the open doors. A young woman hailed another who had been absent from our classes for weeks. As we all greeted the returned dancer, the two fell into each others' arms and danced on the terrace to the lyrical tango that accompanied the class inside. Women, like men, historically have danced together to teach and learn the tango. This, though, was a moment shared out of pure delight.

Europeans, principally from Holland, Germany, and Switzerland, usually arrived in couples. They would integrate themselves into a class and then disappear, just when they had come to be expected regularly, after their six-week vacations ended. These people spoke little or no Spanish. They constituted a major source of income for the profesores with whom they advanced with extraordinary rapidity—but with only varying degrees of cobblestone—by dint of days of private lessons. Other foreigners came and went with less clear goals in mind. There was the young French woman who seemed to have arrived all alone with the vague idea of dancing professionally in Argentina. The Japanese veterinarian had wanted to teach tango on the side in Japan but had so fallen in love with Argentina that she planned to stay. She spoke only Japanese and English, and she lived alone, so I often served as translator of her needs. The beautiful and apparently rich Italian girl fell in love with an Argentine dancer and returned to Italy with him to teach the tango.

Other Latin Americans were less frequent visitors. A talented Brazilian danced in tourist shows and often appeared in milongas. His technique was admired, but he was clearly too exuberant—

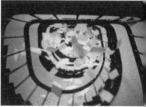

the trait that Argentines expect their happy neighbors to exhibit in contrast with their melancholy selves. This difference is seen as incomprehensible but immutable, the result of a tragic geographic distribution of mood. One night, at the usual good-byes, I felt I had seen one dancer often enough to ask why he gave me two kisses instead of the usual Argentine single parting kiss. "Are you some kind of Spaniard?" I asked, fending off the self-satisfaction that Argentines expect from Europeans. "No," he laughed, understanding the defensiveness. "I'm a Bolivian here studying to be an X-ray technician." In fact, he was the third Bolivian X-ray technician I had met, but he was by far the best dancer.

One evening, a woman I had only just met was sitting with me in a cafe while we waited for someone we both knew. By the time it was clear that the third dancer would never appear, we had told each other quite a bit about our different lives and traded opinions about other people in the tango world we shared. Nuria's face radiated as she recounted how she and other young dancers had barely managed to put on a show to represent their experiments with the tango as a genre. They had felt that the classical ingredients of the tango, different aspects of passion, rage, friendship, and betrayal, had different meaning for their generation; so each participant choreographed one of these key elements. From this had emerged one-person and three-person tangos as well as the usual couples. A young saxophonist provided accompaniment without pay. The night of the performance finally arrived. The theater, which they could barely afford, was without electricity. Nuria and I had to make out the results of their labor of love on an impossibly murky tape several days after our chat. Even in its shadows I realized that most of the dancers were people I knew from practices.

We spoke as well of the reasons that would give me the patience and the interest to sit through the shadowy record of such an obscure effort. I explained something of my own dance history and of my studies. Nuria sparkled again. "This is what I love about the tango," she said, her face illuminated by intellectual curiosity. "I did my university studies, too." She hesitated an instant and then looked at the wall while she added, "I earned my way by dancing in *revues*. But in the theater and the university I never met the people I meet in the tango." Then she continued speaking to me pensively. "You, for example, are so exotic."

Argentines and foreigners alike often asked me disbelievingly, "And you go *alone* to these places?" Not only did I go alone, but so did other women, in numbers large enough that we always outnumbered the men in practices and in most classes. I felt a little different about attending the milongas alone. Milongas are almost always held in a space that not only is a dance hall but also is set up and functioning like one. If a hall is used for a class previous to the milonga, its transformation is quite clear: The lights go down, waiters start serving drinks, bags containing shoes, tights, towels disappear mysteriously, couples arrive. Women and men

continue to arrive alone, but they are fewer in number, particularly the women. An added factor for women, and particularly for me as a foreigner who never adapted well to porteño schedules, is the hour. If you arrive early at a milonga, between midnight and two, you are guaranteed some room on the dance floor. If, however, you are interested in participating in the dance as a social function, either to meet people or simply to mill about in the crowds that porteños so love, a good time to arrive is two or two thirty, something that made many of us think twice and feel constrained to taking taxis rather than public transportation. Nevertheless, women moved about in this tango universe with striking freedom. And we agreed that we faced a reasonably clear-cut situation: People used the classes and practices to dance; a milonga could be used for a *levante,* literally a pickup, and it is the men who look for the levante. Knowing this, women could decide what made them comfortable: Classes and practices that are reasonably egalitarian, and milongas that are not.

An Invitation to the Dance

The milongas taught me the hardest lesson, without exception, that I, as a foreigner in Argentina, had to learn: the rules of the *cabeceo,* roughly, a nod, a ritual and wordless communication between a man and woman across the dance floor. Harder for me than any difficult dance step, the gesture is a face-saving device during which an invitation to dance a set can be negotiated between a man and a woman at sufficient distance that no one else need ever know who asked whom and who refused whom. With the women still sitting around the edge of the floor, the men, from across the room, catch the eye of a possible partner and nod to one side. The translation is not difficult, as the nod would be recognized in many other parts of the world as saying, "Let's go," with different degrees of humor, irony, apology for the rudeness, or simple preemptory command.

At my very first milongas, at country dances during a period when the tango was not danced in the capital, I never made it on to the dance floor. My friends, perplexed, scrutinized my behavior only to find that whenever I found a man looking straight into my face, I immediately lowered my eyes. In a concerned fashion, the women around me explained that I needed to hold the other person's gaze to transmit acceptance of his invitation. This proved far more easily explained than performed, we discovered: Dropping my eyes was a reflex I did not know how to control. Only after careful concentration in the midst of the laughter and disbelief of the other women was I able to fix my stare such that a dance partner would begin toward me. At this point, to my relief, I could look down in order to extricate myself from conversations and table legs and begin to make my way to the edge of the dance floor. My problems were not over, however. So fragile is the agreement forged by only a glance that it dissolves at the slightest indication that one party

might have repented during the time it takes to cross a room. To my bewilderment, the men would almost reach my chair, only to turn and walk away, apparently quite nonchalantly. Again, my friends conferred bemusedly and then grilled me on each move I had made and each word I had uttered. Again, they were able to diagnose my gaffe. As the men had reached my side, I had politely murmured "Gracias," which in this context, as with food and with mate, means "Thank you, no."

After the imperceptible cabeceos, women rise magically in waves around the dance hall, eyes level and backs straight, to move, as though underwater, toward partners unidentifiable to any but themselves. If they or their partners have attended classes and have just come from a practice session, the first dance at the milonga begins the day's seventh hour of tango. A famous tango dancer and profesor once described his schedule to me: "I teach private lessons from one to four, then I come to class from five to eight; I go to practice from nine to midnight; and then—like the postman's holiday, no?—I go to the milonga to rest."

Tangos de papel

Here we will sing, así no más,
the tangos of the exile of Gardel.
And we will recount, así no más,
the history of some paper tangos.
The tangos of the exile of Gardel
are tangos that are acted out in life—
tanguedias that never come down from the marquee.

. . .

We will begin
with letters of exile and of our country
. . . Letters of exile come and go,
bringing us emotions like daily bread:
errands and news that give us
the proof that everyone is still there.

. . .

These notes try as well to recall San Martín
    and the exile of the great unfinished nation.
All Latin American peoples have lived exiled
    inside or outside of their land.

. . .

Exile is absence, and death, a prolonged absence.

Who amongst us has not died a little?

The country we left no longer exists.

. . .

"How did it occur to you to make a tanguedia, as you
     call it?"

"He said to me, 'If you play the saxophone, stay here
     in Buenos Aires. But if you play the tango on the
     bandoneón, go to Paris.'"

"What am I going to do in Paris?"

"The tanguedia. The Exile of Gardel."

"But what is the tanguedia?"

"Something that tells what is happening to us here in
     Buenos Aires."

"I said to him, 'But that is an enormous risk. . . .'"

"He said, 'The decision to be is always a risk. To live
     in Buenos Aires is a risk. But to leave is also a
     risk. The triumph is to hold out, to remain united
     here as well as there.'"

And so his strategy of risk began to develop: It is
     necessary to invent a culture, a poetics of risk.

     —from *Tangos: The Exile of Gardel,*
     by Fernando Solanas

My story shares with other Argentine stories a beginning in
the middle classes and a coming of age at a deeply violent
moment in Argentine history. The way that the middle

classes were caught up in this moment marked Argentina and marked the tango. But neither this moment nor its violence are the only experiences that Argentines bring to the tango. Each different Argentine and I myself think our own different tangos. So, evoking the one individual case I can best know, my own, is better by far than dissecting the ways Argentines see their lives through this dance and its song. My case is not only highly individual but ultimately that of a foreigner in Argentina. Precisely because of this, it illuminates, again by parallel, the way Argentines can think about their own stories with their tango, at different historical moments, under different pressures, from different places in Argentine society. Sometimes these stories come out into the open. Other times they are kept behind a casual and humorous irony: Once an architect said to me as we began to dance, "Well, here we are, supposedly cultivating our national heritage."

The arrival in the United States of two new statements of the tango, the film *The Exile of Gardel* and the Broadway sensation *Tango Argentino,* provided a special focus of self-reflection for expatriate Argentines in mid 1987. *The Exile of Gardel,* in which Argentine exiles in Paris sing and dance out fragments of their broken lives, was directed in 1985 by Fernando Solanas, his own exile recently over. *Tango Argentino* displayed a history of tango dance and song that proved to be a surprise international hit. For Argentines outside of Argentina, *Tango Argentino* brought together their most evoc-

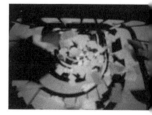

ative tangos and became a statement both of their unique heritage and of its emotional and artistic hold on audiences worldwide.

Expatriate Argentines insisted that I see *The Exile of Gardel* and took care that I meet singers and dancers from the review. The film's *tanguedia*—with its paper tangos and letters of exile—like the classic tangos themselves, has no end. All call for a response that in itself is a cultural configuration of thought. Argentines recognize the danger of self-indulgent reflection as inherent in the tango form and in its related responses. But it is the form and its responses—related meditations on exile, identity, cultural vitality, gender, and the various forms of death—that I am exploring, not by analysis of the form but through an enactment of a response.

All of this, then, is what I think at the same time that it is what I have learned I should think when I hear the tango. But this mix of the profound and absurd that Argentines recognize as appropriate reactions to tango music, song, and dance, implies, beyond shared reality, highly personal experience. Tangos are as different as listeners. But tangos, particularly this canon of tangos, present parameters for thought. The tango mines certain experiences and poses certain unanswered questions, but it does so in the context of certain lives and certain historical moments. The tango and these tangos are ways of thinking about individual lives. They helped me think through my life, as I understand the tango often does for those who take it seriously.

A Paper Tango, 1986

For many years I have been sending and receiving letters of exile; as I write this, the last has come under the door: I do not want to open it. Under the door, the way letters come in Buenos Aires. I am writing this letter of exile for you who told me of a film of exile that speaks of the fate abroad of the tango, your song of loneliness and frustration, written after one exile, during another, and before yet another. These letters of exile are paper tangos. Paper tangos form tanguedias rather than *tragedias;* they are parts of other tanguedias that will never find an end while our children confront yet another exile in their life without a country—like the rest of the world, but our glimpse of our exile, fragmentation, lack of form, and lack of an end to our story came early.

You made enormous efforts to contact me about *The Exile of Gardel,* but because we could find no time together, it was alone that I finally screened the tape. It seemed, nevertheless, particularly appropriate to be alone as I watched image after image of person after person turned thing by the denuded solitude of exile. This is the exile of the tango, the song to loneliness, the exile of everything deeply Argentine, the exile of the solitude of the South. But the song has sung of an exile not only outside but also inside, an exile that already existed before the exile: The exile left his country for the third time when we left Argentina. Foreigners in the New World, suddenly frightened and alone in Argentina, leaving it for a while

or forever for someplace safe. As children of immigrants unsettled in our lives or selves, Argentines find themselves in exile three times distant from themselves, and they can no longer remember when they did not exist in an enormous tunnel of mirrors. I had been caught in it, too. I made notes. I had to write very rapidly: With no time to stop to recast phrases to speak of "them," the notes, like the film, talk of "you" and of "us." Or they are fragments without subjects, where "the tango," and "letters of exile," and the parents and "children of exile," and the exile itself are presupposed to exist in the context of Argentine experience that we share and in reference to those who do not understand but on whom we depend for media, space, and the confrontation of their misunderstanding in order to express ourselves.

I took the notes home. I looked at them just like that, as the film says, *así no más,* on paper. And así no más, I saw suddenly that they were and were not my own life. With the difference that I went to Argentina to study its culture and, passing for an Argentine, I confused even myself. At first we were all students, I just one among many who were exploring an Argentine identity that posed to us problems that often were startlingly the same. The university closed the night I arrived, and we formulated our questions together. Everything I heard served me finally, as it served you, to analyze, again with the difference that this was not only my personal life but my professional task. Yet, after ten years surrounded always by Argentine life, slowly on the edges of my mind my analysis became my experience. And so I studied the tango, but also I danced it in the provinces and I listened to it in the capital and then I used it as a language to think and communicate my experience that was both Argentine and not.

I, like you, lived years when the only continuity consisted in receiving and sending Argentine letters in their airmail envelopes striped sky-blue and white. Like many of you, I studied abroad, in Oxford, with Argentines and taught by Argentines, all of us bringing our minds to bear on Argentina. Like many of you, I also married a member of a community that called itself foreign, regional, and Argentine, all at the same time. Tied to the Asturian Patagonian Argentines, I struggled to keep contact with Hungarian Argentines and Jewish Argentines and English Argentines who "came from" the capital: porteños. Or perhaps it was only our enormous families that kept us apart. I was the only one of all our friends who did not have the backing of such an identity, and so I myself wanted my child to have the only point of departure of which I could conceive: We returned to Buenos Aires so that the child of two foreigners with flimsy documents would be born on Argentine soil, by law irrevocably Argentine. Argentina was our country, Patagonia, our home where the child was taken to "know," *conocer;* but our work, like that of almost everyone else, took us "outside," *al exterior.* So all of us began again to write letters from different points on the globe, and we met in London, in Los Angeles, in Mexico, in the airport in Rio, in congresses in Paris, in order

to exchange *dulce de leche,* caramelized milk, in its blue cans, Sugus candies for the children, and shoes for letters and photos that began their long journey back. And, carrying dulce de leche, Sugus, and shoes whose leather, above all, permeated our suitcases with Buenos Aires, we came to know friends and uncles and grandparents and great-grandparents and children of Argentines in Asturias, in Italy, in Valencia, in Miami, in Rochester, where other photos were on show in which children already grown had once looked at a camera from Tucumán, or Río Gallegos, or, of course, Buenos Aires. Bit by bit the interchange began to include rumors and memories and fears of terror in the country, and for all of us, in our minds flickered moments of fear that had touched us in Buenos Aires: When someone stopped momentarily, in the gesture of serving wine, as the sound of machine guns reached us—and then without knowing what to do, continued serving the wine in silence; or when there was no more news of a friend.

Sometime in those years, as I came and went from Argentina still asking the same questions—sometime in those years I stopped expecting answers, although always expecting letters, from Argentina. This, a second exile, began for me as it had begun for others in other years and other generations. For me and for other Argentines, who had been children of immigrants, the second exile came after a first. In the first exile our families had left one reality for another reality in Argentina. They still spoke of this. The second exile in Argentina itself was the growing consciousness that

Argentina did not offer a reality: Argentina itself reflected back to us our doubts. The tango of the film and the tango in Argentina sing to the vast doubt, the *sinsentido* of the culture—which, as it negates, can also affirm the task of inventing life anew, offering all possible options and with them the exhilarating sensation of crisis. It is, I used to say, a culture of doubt; we needed to build monuments to doubt. In the film, as in the third exile, where we are alienated in many painful physical and geographical ways from Argentina itself and even at times from each other, our culture has become one of risk—the risk that the exile always relives, searching for a reply, an ending that may not exist, inside or outside Argentina.

So we were all exiled two times, and then three. Each of us confronts yet another exile in our children: What does my son remember of Buenos Aires? When will he return? What will it be like if he speaks in a language other than the Spanish I speak to him? What will I tell him when he learns other words, another history, another music? But then all Argentines have always learned "another" language, "another" history, "another" music. With immigrant histories so close, the languages and histories and musics left behind are still heard and told and sung. And in a nation that depends on powers outside its borders, the languages and histories and music of the powerful are also constantly heard and learned. For all of us our exile is our mirror.

All of this is in the notes. But what can I do with

these notes, these reflections in another mirror where I suddenly see myself and you? Now we are no longer students. Now I ask questions of the questions that we posed together. We are perhaps no longer looking for the answer together. If we are not, what right do I have to say that I understood what I have just seen? My dilemma, my life, is the continuous frustrated attempt of the exiles, like us years back and like the film today, to get a dial tone in the public telephones to speak from Paris to the River Plate. I have been in those telephones in Paris. One said, in blue letters over French graffiti, in the booth in 1979, Las Malvinas son nuestras.

Tango Argentino: "Ballad for My Death"

Tango Argentino confronted us with many of the most beloved tangos of all, performed one after the other and culminating, surely not by chance, in "Ballad for My Death," a quintessential Argentine reconstruction of a unique individual confrontation with life.

Why should it be that the sense the tango makes has become so urgent to me as a person? Sometimes I think that I recognize myself in you because you first recognized me. How otherwise did it happen not only that for the most part I was mistaken for an Argentine but that when I received any notice at all it was because one or another or whole groups of you thought you saw in me quintessences of yourselves? At the very least you remembered a model you thought you must have seen somewhere recently or, as often, a doll that might have existed in your past. Sometimes you realized, apparently quite suddenly as you made an aside that I was not supposed to overhear, that you recognized what had always been for you the ideal face. Others felt it clearly natural I ask about the tango as, you concluded time after time, I had the appearance of a dancer. Sometimes an anonymous person who did not quite comprehend what it was I was doing would nod in grave accord that it made sense to study Eva Perón because "you even look like her." More sophisticated acquaintances would make a joke of this, or only tell me much later. Children still blurt it out to my face. Even worse, acknowledgeable now only because none of these experiences will ever occur again, were the repeated times in the provinces and even in the capital when people would expect me to know what to do when they, fishing in the past and the present to understand what it was I evoked, would finally exclaim that they were seeing again just one more of the images of the Virgin Mary that had peopled their lives. I still carry with me the religious medals given to me because they looked like me. I don't know what to do with them.

What kind of curious concatenation of physiological and psychological happenstance could have allowed this to occur? Perhaps the physiological coincidence would never have been noticed had it not been for the psychological circumstance: I was happy in Argentina. People told me my radiance evoked images of madonnas, of Evita who looked like them, of models, of dancers, and of dolls. And to this anoth-

er physiological accident added: at twenty-one, I seemed to the Argentines to be fifteen at the most, and at twenty-six, they guessed I was eighteen. People treated me accordingly. Possibly this would have happened to me in any country— possibly. I can only know that when it did happen to me, it happened in Buenos Aires. I was a favorite child of the city: It was the only moment in my life when merely by existing (in Argentine Spanish, one *is* existentially—*ser*—rather than temporally—*estar*—a scholarship holder; and at the same time, sometimes to my woe, one *is* a doll or the ideal girl-child woman), I was continually *regalada*, "given." People gave me banquets and gifts and offers of everything from flowers in the street to marriage.

So I recuperated a childhood that I never had in my country, what seemed a rather distant place that had never after all claimed me as its own. I could be taken in by family after family that fed me and dressed me and showed me off until I melted into one final family and disappeared.

As anthropologist, girl child, and madonna it was perfectly expectable that I should not know details and rules of earthly matters and that I should need instruction in them. So for a very long time, very many people who I knew I did not take seriously on one level laughed at what they admired but knew could not last, my simplicity. "This is wonderful," I was told once upon breaking yet another bit of protocol of a rather formal culture. "You are totally uncivilized."

The less attention I paid to rules the more they liked it— to a point. At that point they gently took up the task of my education, because, after all, although I might be uncivilized, I was asking for education in their culture, a culture that knew I could not grow up without learning the rules, someday. Among the first things I learned was that I was by nature educated and refined, something recognizable in my mere physical presence and mannerisms. Stripped of the credentials of Harvard, Oxford, Fulbright, I carefully and literally took note that education is not learned, it is taken in with mother's milk, and that what nature does not bestow, Salamanca cannot make up for.

And then I learned that certain political responsibility, certain family loyalties, certain human goals and expectations would be attributed to me as an adult. No one had ever gotten around to this in my own country—or perhaps I paid less attention there where I had not been a successful daughter and where I was not an anthropologist. But when I wanted to take account of matters—*cuando quise darme cuenta*—in Argentina, I was no longer an anthropologist there, either, I was a bride.

Along the way, and perhaps significantly for my new status, my mother had died. She died in California, but I lived out her death in Argentina. I remember the systematic reassurances of the dozens of relatives and acquaintances as they evoked the many deaths they themselves had lived. As I waited to cross the Strait of Magellan and then to continue north, as days ground by in Buenos Aires, my Patagonian family and its contacts searched out a place for me on the

overloaded planes taking Argentine tourists to their summer destinations. On the thirty-six hour flight that would finally take me, landing in Santiago, in Lima, in Guayaquil, in Bogotá, in Panamá, in Tegucigalpa, in Guatemala City, in México—during all this time, I learned not to be afraid, to remember that all children see the death of their parents, to know that there were many people who knew how this happened and what to do. They were waiting for me in Argentina—very different from the bewildered, dumbstruck fragmented little group that my North American family made while it waited two days more for my mother's death, and then dispersed again. Both travel and the death itself seemed to have occurred in Buenos Aires. The last comforting words I remembered hearing were those of an unknowing airline official, consoling me for what she thought was my natural reaction to leaving my country. "May your voyage not be a burden. You will come back to Argentina."

So one by one I learned the lessons of adult life, before it closed over me, in Buenos Aires. The tango reminded me once again that I have lived so much of my life in Argentina that it seems more a state of mind than a country. The tango evoked this time around—in its music and its repeated names of places and experiences taken for granted in Buenos Aires—the sudden realization of human mortality that must come to everyone at some time or in some place.

That realization came to me for the first time—in that sense, really, its only time because afterward I could recognize it—in Buenos Aires. It was in Buenos Aires; it was crossing and going away along a white street; it was crossing Santa Fé, la Plaza Francia a few blocks away in the dark; it was at dawn and at six—everything clear in my mind: the tea house, *el Five O'Clock Tea,* one block from Santa Fé and another from Callao, the last thing I saw before entering the clinic where Martín was born. So that in this sense, in some real sense, I will always die in Buenos Aires just as I will always give birth in Buenos Aires. Other times for me are already imprinted with Buenos Aires. As I listened to this tango I had what must be a primordial sensation of recognizing something profound and commonplace that all human beings must feel but that I happened to feel in Buenos Aires.

> Moriré en Buenos Aires,
> será de madrugada,
> que es la hora en que mueren los que saben morir.
> Guardaré en mi silencio la mufa perfumada
> de aquel verso que nunca yo te pude decir.
>
> Andaré tantas cuadras y allá en la Plaza Francia,
> como sombras fugadas de un cansado ballet,
> repitiendo tu nombre por una calle blanca,
> se me irán los recuerdos en puntitas de pie.
>
> Moriré en Buenos Aires
> será de madrugada
> guardaré mansamente las cosas de vivir,
> mi pequeña poesia de adioses y de balas,

mi tobaco, mi tango . . .

Me pondré por los hombros, de abrigo, toda el alba,
mi penúltimo whisky quedará sin beber,
llegará tangamente, mi muerte enamorada,
yo estaré muerto, en punto, cuando sean las seis. . . .

. . . iré por Santa Fé,
sé que en nuestra esquina vos ya estás
toda de tristeza, hasta los pies.

Abrazame fuerte que por dentro,
me oigo muertes, viejas muertes,
agrediendo lo que amé.
Alma mía, vamos yendo,
llega el día, no llorés.

Moriré en Buenos Aires,
será de madrugada.

I will die in Buenos Aires,
it will be dawn,
the hour of the death of those who know how to die.
I will put away in my silence the perfumed mufa
of that verse that I was never able to tell you.

I will go a few blocks and there, there in the Plaza
    Francia,
like shadows fled from a tired ballet,
repeating your name along a white street,

my memories will tiptoe away from me.

I will die in Buenos Aires,
it will be at dawn.
I will tamely put away the things of life,
my small poem of good-byes and bullets
my tobacco, my tango. . . .

I will put over my shoulders to keep warm all of the
    dawn,
my next-to-last whiskey will not be drunk.
Tangoly, my deeply enamored death will arrive.
I will be dead on the dot when it is six
    o'clock. . . .

. . . I will go down Santa Fé,
I know that on our street corner you are
    dressed in sadness
down to your feet.

Take me into your arms, because deep inside
I hear deaths, old deaths
attacking what I have loved.
. . . Alma mía, let us go,
the day is coming, do not cry.

I will die in Buenos Aires,
it will be dawn.
—from "Ballad for My Death" by Horacio
Ferrer, music by Astor Piazzolla

Buenos Aires. Arbitrary city like all cities. My mother used to say that as a little girl she thought about all those Argentines in her school texts going up and down streets so far away, and she wondered if someday her life would have anything to do with them. Arbitrary city. But seen from Argentina, once there, a definitive point on the map. A point that made itself definitive on my map, the map I bought for my first journey south. That map is now covered with lines, coming and going in and out of Buenos Aires, erasing the city. Is it that my life erases Buenos Aires, or that Buenos Aires became my life? Arbitrary point, but not absurd. Not absurd in my life like Villazón, Bolivia, or La Quiaca, Argentina—where once I thought I might die and where the thought made me desperate at the absurdity of dying for nothing in places that were nowhere to me. It was not that I thought I might die in Buenos Aires: Rather, it was in Buenos Aires that I knew for the first time that I shall die.

Tangos and Violences: Los mareados

Pentimento

> Showing under the finished surface [of an oil painting] indicating changes in the artist's intention or the state of the picture before repair or restoration. They also appear when a surface becomes increasingly transparent over the years, revealing the original underpainting. (Myers 1969, 4:328)

> The sign of a change of mind or concealed mistake by the artist in executing a picture . . . the lower layer begins to show through, revealing the artist's first statement and subsequent change. . . . (Osborne 1970: 826)

> The result of the increasing transparency of the overpainting on aging . . . (Mayer 1969: 287)

> The ghost, sometimes, of one of the children . . . that so often inhabit these scenes. (Mayer 1969: 287)

Repentance; remorse; contrition. (Il *Nuovo Dizionario* 1990: 1936)

There were photos shot at a morgue, of open people, atrocities, and the title of the work was "Bogotá, Colombia, 1990." Then what can you do there?! Nothing! The photographer is not giving an image of Colombia because that has nothing to do with anything!

For meaning to be interpreted, at any level, from the most elementary one to the most sophisticated one, it has to be communicated through the artistic image. If I instead show a dead body to an audience what can they interpret? . . . I swear to you that if it had been her son she wouldn't have taken that photo . . .

In the media they are showing you the particularities of the dead, they are not showing you the dimensions of death . . . those are much richer and doubtless much more profound. . . . I think that art could eventually come to talk about death, and that necessarily implies that you transcend the dead body. . . . In other words, it is very difficult when you are working with blood to give blood a different meaning from the one it already has, blood is already very heavily charged, right? . . . you cannot break the signifier . . . you cannot intervene it . . . you are back to the dead body.

That has nothing to do with the latency of terror.

(Interview of Doris Salcedo, in Villaveces Izquierdo 1997: 250–52)

I was reading the comments of Doris Salcedo, concentrating on her allusions to indirect "revelations," not evocations, of terror through art, knowing that she was working them out in the midst of accelerating violence of Colombia. As I read of the absences and the sorrow underlying Salcedo's work, the tango bled through with its absences and its sorrows. I saw the only too familiar traces of the disappeared and the dead. I began to inscribe a draft of my own on the back of the first page of the interview.

The tango ostensibly sings of lost love. But in my draft I wrote that the tango elaborates on violence and the indirect effects of violence. The tango is one of the ways Argentines have given me to think about violence. I wrote that the tango expresses suffering under terror imposed initially by economic violence that formed the context of the invention of the dance and its songs among impoverished immigrants who did not share a language but who managed to share a dance. This economic violence has been linked again and again in the minds of its victims with the political violence that has caused repeated exiles from Argentina. I wrote that the tango taps this link when it tells of human ties destroyed.

I heard the thickness and darkness of nights of threats, and of unfilled places at tables and in beds. In Buenos Aires, the sound of an elevator at certain hours of the night was enough to make us rigid as we tried to hear whom it had brought and whom they were taking away. As in Bogotá, death came also in the mails and over the night telephone lines. Shoes were left and lost; the dead's vulnerability proclaimed by their bare feet. Shirts were folded and unfolded and folded again in a bitter mix of hope and desperation.

Ruptures added to ruptures. Tango words and tango bodies speak simultaneously to different kinds of brokennesses. The first to be heard is the shattered link between lovers. Because this is the best-known theme of the tango, it is often identified as the tango's "message." Increasingly it has become clear that it is the tango's main metaphor.

> Primero hay que saber sufrir,
> después amar, después partir,
> y al fin andar sin pensamiento . . .
> perfume de Naranjo en flor
> promesas vanas de un amor
> que se escaparon en el viento . . .
> Después . . . ¿qué importa el después?
> toda mi vida es el ayer
> que me detiene en el pasado,
> eterna y vieja juventud
> que me ha dejado acobardado
> como un pájaro sin luz.

First, one must know how to suffer
then to love, then to leave,
and finally to wander without thought . . .
the scent of orange trees in blossom
vain promises of love
that disappeared in the wind . . .

Afterward . . . what about afterward?
all my life is yesterday
that has me detained in the past,
eternal and ancient youth
that left me a coward
like a bird without light.
—from "Naranjo en Flor," by Homero Expósito.
Music by Virgilio Expósito

The disorientation of lost love, so often rendered as drunkenness, becomes the disorientation in the face of a savage order whose coherence and security rips apart human connections, leaving a chaos of aborted relationships, of blighted subjectivities, of broken bodies. Hierarchy, once invoked in the form of the rich man who sweeps the woman away from her lover, now looms as an absolute before which all are impotent, women as well as men. Rules, once twisted by one lover to take advantage of the other, are increasingly seen as the tools of the dominant in the violent repression of the rest of society. The jumbled junk-shop window, *cambalache*, originally from the years of the *crisis mundial*—the

Depression—is one of the most classic images of all classic
tangos.

Que el mundo fué y será una porquería,
ya lo sé,
en el quinientos seis
y en el dos mil también . . .
Igual que en la vidriera irrespetuosa
de los cambalaches
se ha mezclao la vida . . .

Siglo veinte, cambalache
problemático y febril;
ël que no llora no mama
y él que no afana es un gil.

That the world is and always was a mess,
I already know,
in the year 506
as well as in 2000 . . .
Just like the disrespectful window
of the pawn shop
all of life has been mixed up . . .

Twentieth century, pawnshop window
problematic and feverish;
the squeaky wheel gets the grease
and he who doesn't steal is a fool.

—from "Cambalache," by Enrique Santos Discépolo.
Music by Enrique Santos Discépolo

While tango lyrics speak to the confusion and isolation of former lovers, tango bodies are thrown back into a lovers' embrace that paradoxically can establish the most intimate of links or none at all. It can divorce not only the bodies but also the parts of these bodies from each other. This is a performance of rupture in the same way that it could be—and sometimes is—a performance of tenderness. Dancers in performance do not often choose to perform tenderness, although this is a more complicated choice on the dance floor. Dancers on stage most often perform both control and the splitting off of the limbs—and yet to do this they must loosen the body and make sure that it is whole.

The tango appears to be of the genre of European, embraced dances. But danced by Argentines, it displays differences from its European counterpart. The dancers' steps are explicitly different, although danced in an embrace, but coordination is maintained principally by the male's *marca*, something that has been poorly translated as his "lead." When a male tango dancer pressures the female dancer's back, or signals her right hand with his left, more often than not the marca tells her to do a *figura* entirely different than what he himself is doing. Limbs of both male and female dancers seem to move independently of their own bodies. Torsos remain motionless while legs perform what appear to be com-

pletely unrelated figures. Sometimes a lower leg flashes out in a counterintuitive escape. Even eye contact, when infrequently established on the dance floor as opposed to the stage, is abruptly broken. This embrace can be danced to enact and exaggerate exclusion not inclusion, objectification not intimacy, difference not sameness. In doing so, it mirrors exclusions Argentines are vulnerable to at the hands of Europeans. And because they have taken this exclusion in the teeth, they enact exclusion better than its original perpetrators. Hence, perhaps, the European fascination with the tango. A dance of domination like other European, embraced dances became an imitation that surpassed the original. The European inventors watched the reproduced rejection and ended imitating the Argentine imitation. Europeans imported teachers. They imported hair pomade. But they never got the violence quite right.

In the 1920s and 1930s, France imported massive quantities of hair pomade from Argentina (Collier 1986: 107). Today in Argentina, the use of this pomade, *gomina* and its variants, is considered very Argentine at the same time that there is an awareness that it is "provincial" in the context of world culture. Older men and provincials use it, but younger men and porteños also use other products that produce a modified version of the same look. However, in 1920, the French clearly must have been imitating the Argentines. This, together with the facts that the pomade figures in tango lyrics and that the saying "Riche comme un Argentin" comes from the era of the Argentine playboy in Paris, who would have used the pomade and danced the tango, indicates that the first tangomania occurred in the context of a balance of power that approximated symmetry.

Interestingly, for the later history of the tango versus, for example, the mambo—that particular moment of near symmetry *only* occurred among Latin American nations between Argentina and Europe. The symmetry helps account for the complete integration of the tango into the European world of formal ballroom dance to a degree that no other Latin dance, not even the rumba, was admitted. It helps account later as well, in the context of a changed world and a major asymmetry, for the tango's particular appeal to a France looking for a role as cultural leader of a "Latin" world. In the 1980s, France proclaimed its hegemony at the front of "Latin" culture, and a new tango mania spread from France to the rest of the world. Gomina, then, provides a twist on the ups of an image usually considered only to have downs: the greaser.

Salsas and sambas, beguines and bambas, even the rumba, were relegated to lower ranks on a scale of world dances and only briefly rescued from oblivion from time to time. They were seen to be of more plebeian origins, an association sometimes spelled out as more tropical, less European. Their movement vocabulary, though not always recognized as such, speaks of Africa. The African allusions of tango postures were heavily censored as "indecent" in turn-of-the-century Argentina and Europe. These syncopations, held in

tight embrace and almost-forgotten "breaks" of elegant posture of salon, emerge when Argentines dance the tango with *cortes* and *quebradas*.

Few know that they are dancing their African legacy, a legacy that paradoxically draws attention to itself by virtue of the impossibly complete absence of references to it. Where did the African-Argentines go, people ask sometimes. Were they, these conversations go, quite independent of scholarly literature, sent off to the wars where they were promised freedom but met death instead? How is it that Argentines today do not see them, hear them in the tango? They were disappeared.

When the first opportunity opened for a performance of the revue *Tango Argentino,* its creators, Hector Orezzoli and Claudio Segovia, had been in Europe for some time, awaiting such a chance. In response to the possibility offered by the French Ministry of Culture, the two contacted the dancers they had identified as the best in Argentina. But, ironically, for the spectacle that was later to set records on Broadway, there were not enough funds for the dancers to cross the Atlantic from Argentina to France. "So," a dancer recounted to me, "one day we are all summoned, and we appear with bag lunches in hand. It turned out an Exocet missile that hadn't gone off when it hit target in the Malvinas War was being sent to France for repairs. So we get a free flight, but we all have to sit around the missile all the way to France, sharing our lunches."

So what I have been doing in my long relationship with the tango has been gradually moving toward a core violence, peeling back the gloss to expose disjunctures that in turn speak to broken links and broken lives, not least of all my own. I had wondered why my seeking out of tango practices in Buenos Aires had taken on a dimension so compelling that sometimes I found myself abandoning all other activities to sleepwalk to another shabby dance hall. It seemed at first that in a culture physically expressive of affection, I, as a member of a culture that is not, was simply pulled to a moving statement of that affection among companionable, *tiernos,* serious dancers who accepted me as one of them. One year, my sister managed to tell me on the telephone before I cut her off that she remembered seeing my father over many years frequently beat me until I fell. What little I recalled from that conversation made more sense of what could have been a simple search for physical closeness. Until one night, I looked at one of my partners and realized with the same clarity with which I could see the features of his familiar and kindly face that I was afraid he might hit me. So that was going on, too.

Dancers know that they may dance alone within the couple that the dance constitutes. They also know that from outside they are seen as together. Their skill reflects back on them mutually, and they together solicit approval of those who watch, an audience that is an essential part of tango performance. In this, their alienation was traditionally absolute,

one gender from another, one world from another. Gradually it has become increasingly perceived as shared. Partners still ultimately refer to their lone insights into pain. But some solace derives from the knowledge that these insights would make sense to the person in your arms, ironically providing moments of solidarity in the face of the traditional themes of lyrics that sing of the abyss of distrust between a man and a woman. Soberly, tangueros speculate on whether you dance better when in love with your partner, or not.

The audience can be others as close as those at the dance hall or Others with their gaze fixed on tango from a point as distant as Paris. This complicates the fractile lines that tear the tango apart. The dancers share their loneliness, their loss of contact from each other's world while they share separation from onlookers whose gazes provide the criteria for inclusion in or exclusion from still other worlds. The rejections are related: The first feeds off the second. An Argentine tango couple can enact, within an embrace, the exclusions that the world for which they perform inflicted on them.

Violences are exclusions, and terror, absolute exclusion. It is absolute lack of recourse—to law, to resources, to human support. Living through times that inflict absolute exclusions make it easier to see other exclusions, other ruptures as latent terror.

My experience as a woman in Argentina, relative to the same experience in Europe and the United States, has been one of surprised acceptance and, accordingly, a dignity that

I seldom can feel elsewhere. I have often felt this to be due to the very deep respect accorded to motherhood, a respect that can in turn enhance a professional identity in a way that I do not find in other hemispheres. As a foreigner with the choice to stay or leave, I have watched others subjected to the waves of terror that have come and sometimes gone. Once as I watched, I heard that due to an archaic law, since then struck from the books, the father of my son exercized all rights over my child and over decisions concerning his life. This law usually impinged on Argentine lives when children were about to travel abroad with their mother, in many cases crossing the river to Uruguay, and the required permission to travel, signed by the father, was forgotten at home. In other cases, like mine, it can be called on to support the threat that if the mother does not do as the father's family wishes, the child can be taken from her. I could not turn to the law: This *was* the law. I could not turn to family: This was no longer my family. I could not afford legal advice. I walked from office to office, my tiny terror echoing the storm of violence around all of us in the worst years of repression. An Argentine lawyer deeply implicated in that same repression offered the only help I could find and refused to charge me a fee. North American lawyers demanded half my year's salary to include his solutions in a divorce decree.

In Argentina, the tango, with its many exclusions and mirrors of exclusions, can create a space to reflect on power and on terror. The tango can talk about how to think about these things, how to carry them with dignity and grace, and how to demonstrate the nobility of the human spirit by learning to bear such suffering and nevertheless to dance. All this is part of feeling like dancing. The tango has become a way to explore other experiences of exclusion deeply felt as part of Argentine realities. It is marked by absence, by rupture, by violence—it bears these spores.

Argentines have conflated it with experiences similarly marked by violence that they sense in other absences: in exile, internal and external; in war; and in the letters sent from exile, from jail, and from war. So tangos and letters collapsed into "paper tangos." Like letters in an Argentina scarred not only by censorship but by attrition of public services, tangos are coded messages between two people with the acute awareness that this message may—even probably will—be read by a third. Like tangos, then, letters are a repository of an intimacy difficult to express elsewhere, but paradoxically an intimacy that is expected to be mediated, if not violated. Letters force a different world into that of the recipient, who is often torn between anticipation and dread for that reason—the interruption of the letter to or from exile; the fear of loss announced in letters to prison, breaking the news that the relationship the letter represents no longer exists; the new layer of violence added by letters that spell out threats. The letter itself as artifact, like lost shoes, like folded shirts, in the hands of sender or receiver signals absence, rupture, a story inevitably in pieces.

querido, es que no puedo y sí puedo estar
cuando se regatée el precio de la vida
y el canje de una violencia por otra
y cuando te despiertes con el miedo de niño
al sentir algo detrás de una puerta
dejada abierta como siempre en la oscuridad
Es que no puedo ni adulta decirte que
detrás de esa puerta no hay nada
porque lo peor es saber los dos que
ahí agazapado pulsa un mercado persa
donde se venden vidas, violencia, y hasta seguridad
pero en tal carnaval de pesadilla
nunca nunca se puede poner de acuerdo el precio,
ni saber con quien se está regateando,
ni mucho menos saber si la seguridad viene desde una
muerte o promete una vida
o las dos a la vez

¿dónde estás que no te puedo decir esto?
¿dónde estás que te lo estoy escribiendo?
y si estás al lado mío,
¿adónde va esta carta?

dearest, it's that I cannot be there and yet I
    am there
when bargains are being struck over the
    price of a life
and exchanging one violence for another

or when you wake up with the fear of a child
when you feel something behind a door
left open as it always has been left open in
    the dark
it is that not even as an adult can I tell you that
behind that door there is nothing at all,
because the worst is that we both know that
just there lies in ambush an obscenely bustling
    marketplace
where lives and violence and even tranquility are sold
but in such a nightmare carnival
never never can there be an agreement on price,
nor can one know with whom one, has to make the
    agreement,
much less know if security comes from death or
    promises life
or both at once

where are you that I can't tell you?
where are you that I am writing this?
and if you are by my side,
then, where am I sending this letter?

Argentines have been used to knowing that letters have
been written in a code that will say one thing to the recipient
and another to the outsider that happens upon the letter left
open, the envelope lost, the post seized. Likewise, they are
used to knowing that their tangos send to the world a mes-

sage that intrigues and invites ever-renewed attempts to break its code. While the observing world outside the tango dyad has been fascinated by the possibility of spontaneous native passion (Savigliano 1995), Argentines within the dyad were transmitting their highly formalized versions of constricted European identities that had become uniquely Argentine. In the pursuit of these identities, they had constructed entirely different passions: a passionate desire to comply with the requisites of Europe; a passionate rejection of those same standards; a passionate immersion in a bitterness derived from Europe's rejection of Argentine attempts to imitate their way into a reality about which they are so deeply ambivalent.

As an Other in my own society because of my gender and class, I had increasingly found Argentina familiar and recognizable in a way that did not have to do with its identification with Western high culture. It became a mirror in which I could see my own experience of culture as order and violence. Argentines' own experience of violence done to them through imposed cultural order seemed to leave them no choice but imitation. Their experience in turn allowed me to see similarities with violence done to me that had remained unformulated, unspoken. These insights pushed me to others: As an actor in the Argentine order I increasingly found myself confronting not only the violence done to me by my culture of origin but those that I incurred in the very culture—that is, Argentina itself—that had given me the tools to

perceive violence in the culture into which I had been born.

One tired day far from Argentina, I heard a piano and a violin playing something profoundly consoling that I could not place. The rhythm only was familiar but so deeply known that, as I searched my memory for its source, I became convinced that I had heard its rocking solace as a very small child when my mother played the piano so that I could sleep in another room, with my terror of the dark assuaged because the lullaby let me know I was not alone. My mind was completely absorbed with thoughts of my mother, my infancy in California, my fear and the music's consolation. Then I heard the identification of the piece, which was just fading. A moment of vertigo passed as I absorbed the information that it was an arrangement of a tango. Something primordial seemed to shift.

The psychiatrist in the United States had said that she made a rule of analyzing people in their mother tongue. But in my case, she said, she would make an exception since it appeared to be appropriate to carry out analysis in Spanish.

The lyrical questions I have posed to the tango over the years, when set out before me, questioned in turn their own lyricism. I knew that I was talking about something that had been both profoundly pleasing and profoundly disturbing, something that both rendered me visible and disappeared me at the same time, something that I was afraid to touch for fear I would no longer exist.

I remembered being young enough to be enchanted when Argentines transformed me into doll and icon and feminine ideal. I was enchanted in turn by the memory. But it became harder and harder to maintain the spell, since as an exotic thing I was sometimes hard-pressed to be a human being, too. The comparison had been meant as profound praise, and I had taken it as such. I still take it as such: I loved these people; they loved me; love is complex.

In 1993, one of a crowd of companions suddenly made intimate by twenty-four hours shared while waiting for a delayed flight said wistfully, "I've been thinking that for sure I have seen you before. I've been thinking: it was in the Valley of the Moon in the Province of San Juan." I burst into tears. The province of San Juan is one of the only three provinces I have never visited.

As life had gone on for me in Argentina, some of the violence in such otherwise endearing labels became clearer to me, sometimes thanks to the completely clear vision of my growing son. "I," he said, triumphant at his multiple discovery one day at age eight, "look more Argentine than you. Of course, there are blondes here. But in Argentina most people are not blond. That's why you get so much attention on the street. I'm going to make you a sign to carry that says 'I am well over 30 years old.' *Then* we'll see how much attention you get."

My eight year old and I were walking home through the crowded streets after lunch with a very old friend. My friend's supremely caring nature always reminded me why we had remained so close for so long. A memory surfaced of his continual

deep unease at having to introduce so apparently politically questionable a companion to his friends, all actively opposed to the military regime. He seemed to think that he could make up for his repeated failure to acknowledge my presence by equally repeated accounts of how the same friends had exclaimed over my exotic looks later, wondering who I could be. I never pointed out that the mystery could have been solved by simple social mechanisms of greetings that are almost never omitted in Argentina. I never pointed out that I had had something to say at the screening of a clandestine film that he discussed passionately with the others huddled in the dark, uncomfortable room. I felt I might disappear upon hearing who he, my friend, really thought I was. I realized now, on the sidewalk with my son that I had thought, without knowing I thought it, that this man might hit me if I said the wrong thing. Then the Dirty War had closed over us and no links were left at all.

"I wouldn't want to think," I found myself later saying to a friend, "that my existence has been based solely on a *racismo galopante*—a rampant racism." "Of course not," she answered. But we both knew. Of course not my existence. At least, of course not solely.

The Sad Thought Danced

This perhaps you do not know: that to talk of [the city of] Olivia,
I could not use different words. If there really were an Olivia
of mullioned windows and peacocks, of saddlers and rug-weavers
and canoes and estuaries, it would be a wretched, black, fly-
ridden hole, and to describe it, I would have to fall back on . . .
metaphors. . . . Falsehood is never in words; it is in things.—from
Invisible Cities by Italo Calvino

Monday, July 18—We all seem to have many faces, one
we thought we knew and others unimaginable. When
the massive bomb demolished the 100-year-old
granite of the Jewish Community Center, the city's
sidewalks and souls shuddered with the explosion, and the
search for victims and for accomplices began. Or,
we remembered that it had never stopped. Two
years had passed since the other bomb left a crater
in the place of the Israeli embassy and was attributed to no one. And it had been four years since
the authors of the decade of death even longer ago

had been pardoned. It seemed natural—and terrible precisely because natural—that the new victims be called "the disappeared" once again. The suffering and fright were so close in every sense to the ongoing lives of the busy people on the streets that suddenly the question arose more urgently than ever as we peered into each face, What kind of human being could physically put such a bomb into place? Could say to your face that its explosion had killed innocent people as well?

As well as whom? As well as them? As well as us?

Es como hacer memoria con el cuerpo. To dance the tango you remember with your body. That is why it is not usual or easy to dance the tango when you are very young. You remember how your head used to balance in such a way that your eyes looked out at the world as though from under a very wide brimmed hat. If you are old enough you may even remember putting on such a hat, and how it made you tilt your chin to raise its rim just enough to watch how people stared. To do this your neck must become long, reminding you that there was a time when it did this alone. When your shoulders are set far enough from the imaginary hat, your back, with relief, remembers what it felt like to be beautiful or loved. Work and lies and worry turn from everyday memories to a future you cannot recall yet. You breathe the way your mother taught you, the way you did when she looked at you in a new dress or helped you make up your eyes at the beginning. If you are a man you remember back further, to men who came before you in the tango, who still figure in Argentine imagination in their *chambergos,* the characteristic homburgs, and their *lengues,* the white scarves that fell over their chests. You must never ever crease the lengue. You feel your partner as you did when you danced for the first time, when you still looked ahead, when you were not looking back. You have to remember when you were younger—before the time the last person didn't love you, a time and a person important in tango lyrics and lives. A time when you thought you knew who you were.

Then you learn the steps.

> Tenemos otros 70 desaparecidos. Todos somos judíos, pero también todos somos Videla. Decidámonos.

> We have another 70 disappeared. All of us are Jews, but all of us are also the Junta. Decide. (Placard at a protest, quoted in Bruchstein 1994:3)

So you: What will be the tango you want to dance? Decide. We had been talking of the pitiless destruction of the country, of its cities, of its people—the replacement of projects for the future with the anticipation of an unknown catastrophe. In the face of such a lack of protection, perhaps the only thing that can be said with some appearance of certainty is that one person is a woman and another, a man.

He looked at me and said, *"That* is what it is to dance a tango, *flaca."* Sentiste, decidiste. Elegiste, bailaste. You felt, you decided. You chose, you danced.

We know what it is to search desperately for a son, a husband, a brother who one day left for work and "disappeared": under the mortal blow of those irrational beings who do not know how to coexist in peace, who cannot admit disagreement, who cannot stand differences—ideological, cultural, or historical. We see ourselves reflected anew. (Grandmothers of the Plaza de Mayo in Carloto 1994: 32)

"So it seems the tango elaborates all the elements and all the doubts involved in confronting differences," a dancer had thought aloud some months before the bomb—and those months seemed to have occurred only in relation to the bomb—"in negotiating domination, in managing the physical dimension, in dealing with loneliness within an embrace." We sat relaxed after three hours of lessons. We could sit over mineral water or even wine at a *práctica* when we were feeling extravagant, and we could dance without anyone telling us how. But for none of us was the agenda of the problems that the tango broached clear, nor was their solution. Dancing and learning the tango gave us a chance to approach the problems from different angles, to essay the effect of different combinations, to contemplate a history we knew and a future we didn't. "It has to do with the difference between men and women," the woman went on, "and they *are* different. The tango is their encounter."

How did they teach? How did we learn?

Wednesday, July 20—I have gone back and forth trying to understand the classes. And I am not the only one. We have all discussed at length the question of the extent to which some profesores eroticize the classes, and by implication, the tango. During tango practices, after classes, in the milongas or popular dance halls, we asked each other: Is the tango erotic? How is it erotic? How erotic is it? How erotic should it be? How authoritarian is its eroticism? And how authoritarian is the beautiful, inside and outside of the tango?

Sometimes I, like many of the women with whom I have talked, think that the profesores go beyond some limit we can't define. We argue constantly about this with the men in our classes. Almost all the men give the same version: What women call eroticization could be one way to teach the tango's sensual or seductive spirit, or to open the dancers to this part of the dance's nature. Women on occasion agree in principle, but talk more about inability to perform as they would like to because of, as one young woman told me while we waited for class, "problemas afectivos míos." These women disagree with the men in that they do not feel helped by teachers who some went so far as to call a bit "twisted" or on the edge of perverted—*perversón*. At the same time, some saw them as authoritarian and even military or "fascist"—*facho*—in class.

One evening, an otherwise friendly and antic twenty-year-old hissed at me, suddenly a thin-lipped dictator, "You do *nothing* unless I tell you." In the tango there are moments that a woman dancer can use to her own advantage, but I had missed a breath of a beat in inserting a step. Who was this person in whose arms I found myself? Why was there no escape?

There are very few men, a woman dancer once commented, who can be only men. For example, our friend Franklin. He put himself completely into the dance with each woman, and he enjoyed each moment to its fullest. He left off being a protagonist and merged with his partner.

Profesores made asides—particularly welcome among the women—that discouraged male students from teaching the female students. In class, they frequently discussed the female role in the tango and often repeated to us that the woman had to be the equal of the man, despite the form—in fact, precisely in order to prevent the form from becoming a formula. Yet they were unnervingly contradictory.

"Como pensás tu propia femineidad?" the profesor asked me. How do you think about your own femininity? I looked at him. "Ya es hora," he said. It's about time.

He pointed the remote control at the stereo to prevent the next tango from playing. Half joking he pointed the control at me. "I'm going to change you." Then more seriously, "Don't you notice anything?"

"Yes," I had to admit. "I do." I changed. And I learned.

And yet despite everything, what was being taught and learned was not static. The tango did not give us any rules or a representation of anything. It gave us space to reflect on rules, to despair or to feel our bodies recognize, sometimes with disconcerting solace, the way things are.

Conversation continued among the student dancers. "Something else is going on here," said Ana María, "both members of the couple in tango, man and woman, are looking for a harmony. They talk of fitting together, complementing each other—it takes them beyond their own skins. If not, they say, "one is 'dancing alone,' and that is not tango."

As we put on our coats after class, Diego used to remind me that there was, after all, the autonomy of our balance. He

often appeared, accompanied or alone, around midnight, wandering tall and thin into the dim ochre of some dance hall. A light edge of anger tended to invade the eternal discussions with the men—or was it that I was so afraid of the repetition of some distant anger that I reinvented it every time? This feels quite different from other embraced dances, he insisted rightly but with that tinge of irritation. The *eje,* axis or equilibrium, is the key to the tango. Each partner must maintain his or her independent axis or alignment while dancing. Most important, this allows for the very different steps performed by the two *compañeros.* How otherwise could one manage different partners, good and bad dancers, without discriminating against the less skilled, humiliating them?

But how different could the steps be? Women raised their voices in anxiety when presented in class with two forms of a step usually guided or instigated by the man of the couple, but sometimes

reversed so that the woman could take the initiative. The objections were voiced by the female students: In order to perform this step a woman dancer would have to have an enormous amount of security, a perfect alignment. Others countered that this was no more daunting than what was demanded of our male counterparts. Some of these men visibly suffered under the same circumstances. Women often found their sudden vulnerability endearing. "Of course," the profesor's voice took over, "you wouldn't want to do this to some guy who didn't know the step. He'd be annoyed. You could even make him trip."

A solution that appealed to some people, often younger dancers, was a tango in which the members of the couple held each other only with one arm. Some of us agreed that this seemed less imprisoning, others, only more modern. Dancers argued about who invented a way of dancing the tango side by side, in which the woman dances *al revés*, that is, she performs men's steps so that she and her partner make the same movements. Others experimented with a three person tango. But only the "open" tango was ever seen on the dance floor.

In class one night, a profesor contemplated aloud at length the changes in the world, new complementarities of roles: "It would be difficult to imagine the woman leading—perhaps she can, but it would have to be from her experience as a woman: She could lead *as a woman*. In the future." We were left wondering what this meant.

We had thought we were close to something new when in

a few classes the women had been told to lead the men. When this happened, the extra women in the class had been incorporated in the exercise so that some were set to lead others. We loved it. We had tried this at other moments and talked about it on the edges of classes, over supper afterward in the middle of the night, in cafés when we met outside of the academia. What was interesting was the idea of the exchange of energy. If one dancer felt moved by the interaction or by the setting or by the music to launch a movement, she could smoothly take her partner into the embrace usually reserved for the man, and lead. She could continue to lead, or her partner might immediately change the embrace again to continue into another figure or rhythm. The attentiveness and sensitivity that this demanded augmented our participation and the level of energy to a feeling of exhilaration. Now legitimized by the teachers, we could try this out in the center of the dance floor, and the men would also have a chance to try. The laughter and astonished comments suggested that everyone enjoyed this equally. But once we stopped, possibilities closed down. The instructor asked the men for their reactions and commented merely that now they would know the male role better. A bit taken aback, one of the women, who had not been asked for her opinion, inquired, "And wouldn't this also offer a choreographic possibility?" No, the response came back. This had only served to enhance the men's lead.

One day, the profesor told me that my body was

at times "indecisive," and I finally understood that what he meant to say was that my shoulders and my legs were not absolutely coordinated. I had been thinking about this for several days and had formulated the same problem in my head. Assuming that after several weeks of daily classes we had reached some level of mutual confidence, I dared to ask if the problem could not be that so many flattering remarks—the classic but usually public *piropos* offered by men to women in the course of Argentine life—disoriented me to such an extent that I felt alienated from my own body and could not make decisions with it.

He said, pronouncing each syllable in monotone, "That could be. We will try."

From that moment on, he no longer spoke to me. He made no jokes. He made no piropos. He did not smile. He tried, in some absolutely necessary instructions, to use the formal term of address, but he stumbled over it. I asked myself if I should resort to the interpretation of some of the men: The profesor used a brilliant pedagogy, only to be offended when I did not know how to appreciate it. Was the problem that I had forgotten the remote control and had broken the circuit between the control and my reaction? We danced in total silence an hour every day, with the exception of the minimum of explanation he used to criticize or introduce new steps. One day he taught what was for me a bewildering spectrum of variations on one theme and demanded that I repeat them. I took up the position to start, stating briefly that I undoubtedly could not produce each and every step that I had just glimpsed. "All," he stated. "I want to see them all."

Was I just another *yanqui* who should have gone home? Perhaps some deep absolutism had finally come out in me. Or worse, it could be the culturally specific North American moralism that Argentines routinely diagnose, dismiss, and constantly resent. The Argentines that I knew felt that I was free of this. But how free could I be? I am a specialist in their culture, yet produced by a long and complex series of maneuvers of my own culture. Grant after grant, degree by degree. With my North American moralisms about piropos and my Argentine doubts about the bomb that I was no more able to solve than any Argentine. Piropos had always humanized the streets, made them safe; bombs made them dangerous and marked our lives. I wrote about piropos. I wrote about political violence. Had I now made a colossal professional mistake, a cheap universalist shot at the only particularity that I know thoroughly? Or do I know any particularity thoroughly?

And now I was as terrorized as anyone else with all the same unanswered questions, just cast in slightly different terms. Outsider or insider, I sat on the edge of my bed looking at the telephone, and wondered. Accomplice of a superpower in the midst of the splintering culture that that power was helping destroy? Companion in safeguarding what was left, or at least in expressing it? How could I know what to protect? If I were superfluous as well as afraid, I should go

home. But where would home be? None of my studies, none of my grants had addressed that question. The bomb had made versions of that question once more immediate to everyone on the streets. We heard that they had the answers in the United States Congress where, for reasons that seemed to change every day, the Argentines were called to account. It was the Iranians. But we knew it was we—whoever we were. So I stayed.

He said I had reacted like any porteña in the face of what a porteña might perceive—correctly or not—as an excess of intimacy. I had thought perhaps he would listen if I recalled to his mind that I am a foreigner in Argentina, which might vouch for my lack of intention if I had offended him. "Ah no," he replied. "You can't take refuge in some supposed identity as a foreigner. You reacted like any porteña."

Among the porteñas, in class and seated at the edge of the floor, at practices or actual dances, waiting for the summons of a possible dance partner, we had often warned each other about which dancers to avoid. "Don't look over there," a woman would say with wry amusement. "That fellow will ask you to dance, and he dances well. But he's one of those who will spend the whole time correcting your step, your posture, *and* your emotional adjustment." A row of female eyes would swing to another part of the dance hall and stare fixedly for the moments it took us to try to avoid, for at least a set, yet another man who used the tango to dominate in the guise of teaching, to reproach you, to tell you that you have done something wrong.

"That's the typical porteño for you," a smiling, gentle man said once, when I commented on his extremely cautious politeness in offering a slight correction of my position. "Not only do they not care if you are interested in being corrected, but they blame you for their mistakes." So where was he from, I asked. "Oh I too am a porteño. I'm just a porteño *tolerante*."

I called my friend Mario who I thought might be able to assess the situation. I thought he might have something in common with the profesores del tango because of his own traits as a porteño who enjoys both women and control. He often announced himself wryly as "another hysterical porteño male. But psychoanalyzed." In a previous year, I had substituted for the partner of a very fine dancer, himself a friend of a well-known professional tango dancer. I had thought I was standing in simply to help him stay in practice. Once, I told Mario that I had just danced twelve hours straight with this man, from seven at night to seven in the morning. La Gorda, over eighty, with whom I lived and compared anecdotes and tango techniques, was vastly amused. Mario, less amused, informed me, "Porteños don't go out until seven in the morning just to dance. Something else is going on here." And I probably thought how comfortable it was not to know so much about porteños at seven in the morning in order to continue immune. That's probable. But what is certain is that I did not believe that what Mario had in mind was what in fact every day left me so chilled that I had

to struggle to ignore it, the price that I calculated I had to pay to have so skilled and dedicated a partner. We often stopped after practice and before a milonga to eat something. This fellow, of whom I knew nothing more than that he danced well and was held responsible by a noted tango teacher, would pronounce each evening after a glass of wine, "All women are *putas.*" I imagined that that was *not* the "something else" to which Mario referred. Neither was I going to ask him because I wanted him to reassure me now.

But now, so many years later, my classes were infinitely worse than the worst that could happen on the dance floor. So it was not clear whether in fact they could be just an exaggerated form of dance-hall discipline. "No," I had once answered to a critical remark from another student in the class. "As a dance master he is not unbearably military. Compared to ballet masters, he's a sweetheart, and compared to my father, ballet masters are nice guys." And then I realized what I had said and felt a wave of panic. How much would I take? I quit the classes. I did not stop dancing, but I agonized over problemas afectivos.

Those classes had been so eerily recognizable that I had to ask if I had somehow made a monster out of someone who had never in my presence been anything other than charming, articulate, and intelligent. How had I done this? How could these be different faces of the same person?

Before I had left the United States, I was called as an expert witness in a legal case for a latina family in Texas. Earlier in the year, having just entered what was a new school, the son of the family reported being identified as colored, specifically as "a little brown Mexican shit." This was not new, according to his parents; similar epithets had become increasingly violent over the years. What was new was the added warning: "You better look around you. Everyone else in this room but you is white." The next day fifteen of these white young people attacked the one fourteen-year-old brown person in the room. "But," the administrator asked dismissively, "there hasn't been any aftermath has there?" I explained that the family noticed a total silence coming from their heretofore communicative, spontaneous son. "And couldn't this silence be due," concluded the administrator triumphantly, "to this child's increasing awareness of his own guilt?"

Monday, 13.45 horas. I take a taxi. The driver says, ". . . and besides, a bunch of Argentines died . . ."

Monday, 23 horas. Bernardo Neustadt appears on his program . . . he speaks against the barbarity and says, freely paraphrasing Bertolt Brecht: ". . . today it was the Jewish Mutual Association; the next time it could be us . . ."

Monday, 0.20 horas. Marcelo Tinelli . . . announces that his program, because of its comic nature, will not be aired. . . . He reads

a declaration that repudiates the terrorist attack. In one of its paragraphs it says ". . . and many died who had nothing to do with this . . ."

Questions: Those who weren't Argentines, who were they? Us? Then who are the others: were there victims who did have something to do with the bomb? Had they done something?

But the truth is that many . . . can begin to cross the street in order not to be victims of a bomb with which they "have nothing to do." (Fischerman 1994: 10)

Algo habrán hecho. They must have done something. They must have been mixed up in something. These have become the dreaded or welcomed phrases, deadly words, that Argentines know have been used to disappear disappearances. What did they do, what have they done, to merit such a fate? The questions give logic to the sudden arbitrary absence of a neighbor or workmate or relative, to then dismiss that absence and to render the absence itself invisible.

In the days of the Junta, the police used to call a mother to ask, "Señora, do you know where your son is?" That son was disappeared.

Guille said: You wouldn't be the first who had it happen— who had to leave because of something like this.

Juliana said that she had lived the breakup of all her adolescent relationships in the same silence. Those people had silenced her, punished her. They had silenced everyone different, she said.

The male psychiatrist said: Don't believe that piropos are innocent. There is always an ulterior motive.

The boy on the street said, smiling as he passed me: Just a little longer and I could climb up the braid to win the princess.

Anita, moving among clients in the hair salon, said: A guy and on top of it a tanguero—that's a charged atmosphere. But the kids—the ones on the street—those piropos are innocent.

Another boy said, in what I always recounted as my *piropo máximo*, "Señora, perhaps you could let me be your son." "But I have a son your age," I laughed. "I could be the oldest son," he laughed back. After which he gallantly presented me with a very large bonbon, and my bus swept me away.

Laura said: Show me a man who goes for the tango and I'll show you a machista. They all believe they are Gardel.

The woman psychoanalyst from the provinces advised: What you needed to have done was be more indirect, make a reference to a boyfriend.

Juliana went on to say: In Mexico, or maybe the provinces here, you'd have to find an indirect form. But in Buenos Aires, no. You reacted like a porteña. The problem is that you have idealized too much. You didn't want to see it. You didn't want to see it.

Someone said, shaken: It seems there is something loathsome in this country and then it surfaces.

Guille sat down beside me: If you haven't seen it ever, couldn't it be also that it isn't there?

The question still tormented me: Had I made my own monsters? How otherwise could they be so similar? What had I done?

Has quedado preguntando que habré hecho, she said, triste. Te desapareció. You've been left asking what you have done, she said, sad. He disappeared you.

The worst was, for the moment, I was nowhere to be found.

> Are there *happy cities?* . . . Is a *happy city* an *innocent city*? For many, many who have spoken during these days, yes: Buenos Aires was a happy city and an innocent city. And it is not so. There are nazis here because there have been nazis, there are racists because there have been racists and there are dead because death is and has been one of the means [*modalidades*] of Argentine politics. (Feinmann 1994, 32)
>
> . . . this happy crowd was unaware that . . . the plague never disappears, that it can remain during decades dormant in furniture, in clothes . . . and there can

come a day when the plague, to the misfortune and for the instruction of humankind, awakens its rats and sends them out to kill in the happy city. (Camus cited in Feinmann 1994: 32)

Tangos de papel, bis

o write about the tango, to write about violence has not been writing at all. I have found my own notes in the margins of pages of my own text where I have tried to talk to myself about the feeling I have had that, as I have assembled words on the pages, I am doing something vaguely familiar but not writing. My notes to myself say things about writing as dancing, dancing instead of writing. The notes say that my body has been involved on the pages where I evoke bodily actions or incorporated attitudes. The pages communicate the way I remember my dance masters teaching: The master marks the steps, the others mark them with him. They mark behind his back and just behind him in time. The lag is greater when the steps are more difficult or more unfamiliar. You mark to teach and you mark to learn. I started by marking things that I hoped others would be able to follow. But I found that once my body was engaged, it sometimes marked while my thoughts followed. When I have been able to mark just behind my body, what I

have learned has arranged itself on the page with the same longer or shorter lags that were part of any dance class. Other times, though, the lag has been desperately endless. Like what I remember of triple pirouettes. Like snapping my leg from the knee down in the *boleo* of the tango.

After my days of trying to mark what my body told me, I found that that same body would shake me awake at night with its heart beat, battering my limbs, leaving me thinking that I might suddenly find myself completely disarticulated. It also left me certain that it was marking a pattern that I could not follow, something it knew about me that I would not or could not find out. Something half danced on the pages, and in the words left from the day, something stored up in the dancing body that I can't dance anymore. When my body refuses to dance, it is talking about this. The fact that it compels me to dance talks about it, too. Sometimes I sit up on the edge of the bed to reincorporate all my jittered joints, and I wonder what they know that I do not.

It has something to do with the cloudy understanding that it was through this body that I first conceived of danger and rejection. If as I dance the body is disciplined and beautiful, at least something tells me it is safe. I am reassured to know it is there, it is visible, and that other accepting eyes hold it together like very fine wires. It won't possibly do something all by itself, or maybe worse, dragging me along with it, fall to pieces, leaving an ugly hodgepodge that no one will want. That no one will want or, worse, that no one will see and so cannot even exist.

Actually, from early moments of terror and the rejection that came on its heels I learned that nothing is safe. But throughout my life I have kept this thought at bay. I have done this sometimes by staying at a slight lag from my own body, never talking directly from it or about it. Sometimes I am unable to assume its actions as mine. And yet other times I get hold of it and never let it act on its own.

Early terrors compound each other by being not only violent but secret. I had forgotten about that. I forgot that it wasn't just that I couldn't tell, but that there were people and rules that wouldn't let me tell. Argentina seemed familiar when I first moved there on the night of the coup that caught us all up in webs of people and rules that told us what we could not say. It was a world like the one that had taught me as I grew up to write like a dance and to dance rather than write.

First I wrote letters. The first thing I wrote was a letter in block print to my grandmother. My strange idea was to look forward to leaving the family that was unhappier than I could imagine in order to write letters back about the wonderful life I would lead when I escaped to a world that would no longer reject me as stupid and ugly. I went away and wrote and wrote, into what I considered a personal diary, entries that all took the form of letters. I thought it completely natural to carbon all of these to send in duplicate to my mother and grandmother. So I removed myself slightly from my own experience as I continually coded it into letters.

After my grandmother died, I continued making one copy for my mother. After my mother died, I stopped writing. I had no one for whom to recode her death or my life, and I could not bear her death or write my life out of code.

In the meanwhile, I had perfected another code: my Spanish. It was part of my job after all, which was to learn about Argentines and Argentina. So I marked their words, just as I marked their lives—the way I had learned to mark the steps of a dance master, until I learned to do so—to *mimetizar*—with such perfection that my experiences, my gestures, and my language seemed indistinguishable from theirs. Since I could not think of my own life and language, I did not—and nothing seemed to be in the way of the new patterns. The match was so perfect that I did not notice that I was again at a slight remove from what was happening to me and that I could hope that I was safe once more. Whatever the danger was, it remained just beyond the structures of the code into which I had cast it. The code was as elaborate a shield as it was successful. I reaped the acceptance of an entire population that would ignore my faults in the face of their amazement that I could replicate each idiosyncratic turn of phrase, each specifically appropriate expletive, apparently all different and intricate forms of slang. I also could hold up the shield, firmly in place, when I spoke of intimacy. So I formed a new family where I *never* spoke my native language, not to express affection, not to express anger or frustration—the latter causing astonishment even in bilingual and trilingual Argentine families I visited with my growing son.

This situation was all the more baffling to the people we encountered in the United States, where I returned for my work. As years went by, punctuated regularly by visits to Argentina, whenever deeply distressed I found a refuge in writing out the problem, in something like the way I solved intellectual problems in academia, but always in Spanish, with the thought that in this way no one would understand the piece of paper should I drop it by mistake someday in one of the endless waits in offices where I often wrote. After years of this scribbling I suddenly wondered why I cared if anyone who found my lost notes would understand them: how had I thought they would know whose secret they had found?

> miré las caras tangueras
> dos
> distintas, angustiadas
> distantes de sus pies tan juntos
> y tan intricadamente sincronizados
> y supe
>
> así que por una vida hemos estado bailando
>   el tango después de todo
>
> cada uno por su lado, sin tener la menor
>   idea de qué hace el otro
> igual como que nos escribiéramos cartas

todas esas cartas
  all those letters that went
  into a black hole
  al morirte me dí cuenta
  no habías recibido ninguna
  ¿mamá?

ninguna carta
  vos que no escribías y no sabías hablar
  de vos reclamo el derecho de extrañar

  y de perder

  amorcito

todos esos años enmarcados de cartas
  por las estampillas sabía de donde las había
    mandado
  y sin embargo
  queriéndote tanto
  nunca sé donde estoy yo

  argentina

tan parte mía que cartas sobran
  hasta ahora
  cuando comienzan las distancias
  no tan grandes para escribirte
  todavía
  no tan pequeñas para hablarte
  ya

hijo lindo

de mi cuerpo

de mi vida

¿tu cara? está junta a la mía?

y ¿nuestros pies?

When I began my tango classes ten thousand kilometers away from my birthplace and my ballet lessons, I wondered if my body, initially so foreign to the music and movements, would prove indecipherable to the tango maestros. They knew nothing of me, and of course the etiquette of the dance prohibited us from speaking as we danced.

The moment I felt most irremediably foreign in Argentina, I was waiting for a tango to begin as I started yet another class. The first beat sounded, and I saw and felt the expert dancer incorporate that beat with a look and a movement that I could not fathom. I realized I could not even hear the music as it sounded to others in the room. I was overwhelmed. I was deaf. Would I ever hear that music? Would I ever dance it? This suddenly infinitely distant person put his arms around me and began to dance. I had spent over twenty-five years studying his country, ten of them right there in his city.

That had already been a bad day. I had been unable to recognize myself in the mirror when I looked out of the corner of my eye during the lesson in the mid-February heat in the dim studio. The figure in the mirror could not move. In fact,

that had been the worst day of all. But I had had other bad days. Any partner could tell me, before I had formulated it myself, that something was wrong: *el nerviosismo,* the rigid muscles that he attempted unsuccessfully to cope with told him. They told him more than I could have, even if we had been permitted to speak. When we separated, he would sometimes offer a short condolence, acknowledging that it wasn't my fault, that everyone had bad days.

Once the seizure was so painfully clear to both of us that my partner laughed as he enfolded me in his hug to the bemused staccato of the conventional greeting, Hola-amor-qué-hay-de-tu-vida. The combination of the standardized and the heartfelt startled me into dancing, and the lesson began anew.

I was stepping off an edge into another substance, where boundaries and nerves dissolved slightly. They dilated. My skin was somewhere else. "Where," the maestra asked, "do you look for the sensual? You can look for it, you can dance it in very different ways. Through tenderness, through energy, through anger, through the erotic." Categories dilated again. They overlapped.

We had come to take each other into account in an intricate way, a way that involved our bodies. The physical had been, after all, our initial mode of knowing each other. It was in some ways an idiom, the idiom of the streets where, like streets anywhere, we might hear ugly things but where we were more likely in my experience—but not in the experience of my friend Estela who longed for the streets of Belgium—to hear something that reassured us that we shared the city with other human beings who recognized us, inevitably men and women, whether gay or straight. Dancing in the arms of each other, we each regained bodies we had lost, some of us in our histories, others in the days at work or in families, before we stepped onto the dance floor.

And who controlled whom, finally? All the women were on guard against dominating men. They were a problem in the tango as they were in our jobs and families. My wariness of them called into play yet another problem of control, often encountered by tango dancers upon first arriving from another world. Many women and some men found that it was we ourselves who exercised the control most difficult to loosen. "Avoid thinking," we were told. This happened so often that a serious Swiss dancer, called upon to explain why she continually repeated a particular mistake, painfully analyzed in careful Spanish, "I was thinking, and that is very bad."

But clearly we were meant to think and to search. The problem was conceptualizing movement on its own terms: "You must take care," the maestra once explained, "not to repeat in order to memorize the steps in your head. If you do that you will dance automatically. In the tango you mark steps in order to become sensitive to the music and to the particular circumstances of your partner at any given moment. And all moments will be different. You must remember how the step felt, not what the step is."

With our partners, with the music, we were meant to feel a transmission direct to our bodies, not through our heads. "Your partner feels you resist," the profesora went on. "If you think the step and try intellectually to define it, he thinks you are dancing alone, *bailás sola.* One thing is not knowing what the step is. Another thing entirely is that your body might not know how to do the step. A partner registers *that* as just that, and he does not feel you resist."

What I did in the face of this new idea was shut my eyes, something I thought would allow me to concentrate better, as it had other times. I had the strong sensation that things went better, but when I opened my eyes, I had trouble anew with the steps and with my body. Yet, I couldn't identify what it was I saw that was so troubling. What had it been that I did *not* see? "Perhaps," the maestra suggested, "you're like children who think 'Nobody can see me' when they have their eyes shut." As I turned this over in my mind, I discovered aghast that what I was seeing with my eyes open was not her feet, not mine, not her body—I was searching her face to see some sign of approval or its lack. This was what I was not seeing when I shut my eyes.

A teacher had been looking at a magazine while I danced and then had left the room. When the tango finished, he walked back in and casually remarked, "The problem as I see it with you is this. You give yourself so little permission. You don't listen to your body. You force it into your idea of the step, and your body shows you that that choice is impossible. The step is wrong. Your body is right; give it permission."

One day, going down a list of comments on the different dancers in a large class, a teacher routinely addressed me, "And you. A docile body is not a submissive body. In the tango the woman's body needs to adjust itself—*adecuarse*—to the man. But you sometimes perform as though you think that if you don't do a step well, the man will kill you. Eso no está bien."

She thought a moment. "For some of us it has to do with what centuries of women have been taught. We don't learn what men want. We learn to anticipate men's desires. But if you anticipate the man's *desires*, you are dancing without *him*."

For the man the paradox was different. He might dance well, but even as he did so he could be dancing out his isolation. One of my youngest friends once asked if I, as an anthropologist, might be able to help him solve a problem: When he had studied English in the United States in a program for people from all over the world, he and the one other Argentine in the group had gone longingly to gatherings of the Latin students. But, they found to their bitter dismay, they could not dance like the others. "Why not?" he asked me again and again. One day I, with his question repeating in my mind, stood stunned by the answer I was hearing in my tango class: "Neither in the entire inventory of folkdances in Argen-

tina, nor in the tango, do dancers move their hips." Here, the instructor demonstrated the absolute maximum hip movement for the traditional samba, a delicate movement that I at least needed to be alert to catch. "For the Argentine man, in contrast with men of the rest of the continent," the minilecture continued, "to move the hips is effeminate. And so, the hips and shoulders are 'armed' as a unity." We all looked at each other, chilled, many women hurt by the exclusion, foreigners and Argentines alike not wanting to remember that in traditional Argentine culture, those "men of the rest of the continent" were classed as black and brown to their white. Other people's hatreds were encoded in my friend's body, part Jew, part Indian, part Spaniard—habits so impossible to shed that they were worse than any tattoo.

So, as women, we were taught that we had to learn to dance with these complicated men in a dialogue. We had to listen to them, to the music, to parts of Argentine culture that we did not want to think about. Gracielita, whose terrifying father had been reduced to pleading with her to save him from the hospital where he eventually died, said that learning the tango was in many ways a debt to him that she was still paying off. Azucena, whose father had never touched her after she was eleven or twelve, always thought of him and of herself without him, she said, as she danced. La Mireyita, who began to dance within a week of her young husband's death, was like her father, the communist who had come young from Europe and who learned to play the cello when his wife died in order to play a requiem. The

Requiem-no-sé-qué. But we had never asked each other outright why we were dancing.

It is up to the woman how she moves her body. The dance needs both dancers' emotional response to the music. The woman listens to the music "in stereo," since she has to be aware as well of the man's interpretation. One of the major modes of expressing her own interpretation is through the ornaments, embellishments that are slipped into the standard steps and figures. How to use them, we were told, is a search that is undertaken by each person according to what they want to say: to speak of pain, of happiness. "You could decide to make your legs cry, or laugh. A leg can weep."

Too, we could learn to shake the men out of repetitions. If you startle your compañero within the terms of the dance— that is, he should not fall down—he would have to find a way to resolve the dilemma that you suddenly posed for him. You can steal the step; you can do it backward; you can hook his foot with yours and drag it unexpectedly; you can move up almost into his face. Lo tiene que resolver o pasa el papelón de su vida.

Everyone in the school knew that I had notorious problems with the embrace. The problem is not unusual; but for me it was particularly difficult. It was more than the embrace—*el abrazo:* It was the handing oneself over into the embrace. *La entrega. La puta entrega.* My class on the entrega went like this: The teacher had me sit on the floor in front of the dancer who was my partner while we were to follow

the inscrutable orders of dancing an entire tango "with the gaze [*mirada*]" and then, without speaking, we were to stand and dance, "and we will see where we will go from there." This was an amazingly difficult assignment, especially as neither of us had ever done something of the sort previously. It was not made easier because another student had stayed after an earlier class and sat watching. We got to our feet and started dancing when, to the initial discomfort of all three, the profesor gave the other woman instructions to dance with us. We made acutely awkward gestures to incorporate each other into movements we had learned as a dance exclusively for two. The other woman withdrew; the profesor danced; the woman returned. We two continued an embraced tango as best we could, which by this time took so much concentration that I only registered the others when they directly impinged on our movement. But this they increasingly did as the different bodies gradually became trampolines, each energizing the other in an unmistakable but completely unexpected way. And I began to feel that I was watching in a waveringly cynical disbelief. My partner positioned the dancer who was myself to bend backward. I know very well I have never been able to bend into a deep *suplé,* and for an instant I wondered what would happen when I went beyond the point I know is my physical limit. But my body's head touched the floor. The teacher was telling me and my compañero to ready ourselves to dance anew to Ute Lemper singing Kurt Weill's tango, which we were hearing for the first time. There was not one missed step or lost beat, not one hesitation, not one moment where the synchrony of the two bodies was broken. I took off my shoes and walked out of the building with the feeling that I had just seen a ghost. I left Buenos Aires days later.

Away from Argentina, I began to dream night after night that I was dancing. I would dance and dance, and the tangos would be interspersed with moments of terrible fear. I didn't know the next step. At that point, I would watch my body make a decision, and it would be right. It would decide again, and again, and again. At first I thought it lucky that I was just having dreams about this and not nightmares about the puta entrega. After two weeks of dreaming these dances, watching them end well and end well and end well, they were suddenly about the puta entrega after all. The problem wasn't handing myself over to the man: It was handing myself over to my own body. I woke up.

One dances one's best always, whoever it may be that one dances with. And one dances with *that* person. I dance to her—to her sweetness, to her intelligence, to her elegance, to her beauty, to her own dance. And you? How do you dance? Those are things you have more or less buried. The tango needs them; the tango needs you—you as foreigner, you as classical dancer, you as mother. . . . Go find them again. Dig them out.

> The sight of bricks, beams, ironwork being lifted away in the search for life reflects our everyday struggle because we are experts at

removing earth and rubble looking for truth. . . . and for those who were disappeared alive who have to be rescued out of the depths [*entrañas*] of evil. (Grandmothers of the Plaza de Mayo in Carloto 1994: 32)

After the rape when I was three or four—since no one ever mentioned it I don't know how old I was—I did and didn't think about it. I did and didn't both, in that order, to manage impossible memories—impossible because I had been too young to define what had happened, impossible because it was somehow linked to a father who could not protect me and hit me instead, impossible because I could not stand what had stayed so long wordlessly in my mind.

So it wasn't exactly the way fellow dancers saw it the night of the day after the bomb over coffee. They had commented that they had been watching me at the cafe table where I had been talking politics and of the problems of racism and anti-Semitism with still other dancers. Those at the other end of the table in turn had begun to discuss "the strength that you must have had to put yourself so much into something so unique to us—coming as you do from a culture where you don't touch, where you don't have intimate friends, where you don't drink coffee at midnight—things we know are strange for you." It wasn't exactly that.

The dancer who told me about this night added, "The questions the tango poses are difficult ones that you will have to answer alone—for me, this could all be linked to your past—your relation with your father, the ballet that you learned as a child, the problems of submission."

In the news Rabbi Plavnik said,

> The police wanted to use the term "missing person"...
> but I said no, I believe that we should use the same
> word that was used for the victims of the dictatorship.
> To kill is to steal a life. But this, which was the most
> terrible calamity that could be conceived, is sur-
> passed by a greater calamity: to steal death . . . from a
> person they steal the life of a loved one and then also
> they steal the body. (González 1994: 15)

After the rape, when I was eight and thirteen and sixteen,
I listened to the mother I could not call walking by the room
where I could not sleep. I listened to her crying in the
kitchen, from my bed with my arms crossed trying to flatten
myself into the mattress. All those nights of guilt. No, I
couldn't think about being touched, about being intimate,
about being close over coffee at midnight. I could only wonder what had happened. I wondered if someone had stolen
my body. The one I had never felt like me. Or was it that the
name that meant me didn't go with that body?

When I was twenty and thirty and forty, I looked back
impassively. Then someone said, "You're hungry," and I realized there was a body that was hungry. They gave
me a piece of bagel and a word of condolence.
Pobre. Suddenly I realized they were talking about
me, and I felt sorry for the first time for that small
long-ago body. The person with the bagel had recognized a me. But when the bagel and the person

were gone, when the word did not repeat, the body shattered
and disappeared again. It reappears fleetingly in the tango.

bailando el tango sin vos
me enseña
que por lo menos me hiciste sentir
lo que me hacía falta
lo que no me podías dar
lo que nos separó
En los brazos de otro
se puede tener la seguridad de estar acompañada
los brazos realmente están ahí
y mientras no me sueltan
puedo pensar
lo que nadie me dijo
lo que nadie me dejó pensar
¿te dejaron así de sola y lastimada?

pobrecita
no me dijieron
pero como sí dicen, y como sí me dejaban pensar
estamos en el baile, bailemos.
Salvo que para mí ya era ese carnaval terrible
donde no sabía quién vino con máscara.
Tenía mucho miedo, y fué muy difícil bailar
a pesar de ser bailarina

a pesar de y precisamente porque
como también dicen

nadie te quita lo bailado
ni del tango ni del carnaval enmascarado

Because of this, in this terrible circumstance in which
we find ourselves, the Grandmothers of the Plaza de
Mayo suffer, understand, and accompany . . . assuming the commitment of demanding Truth, Justice, and
Never Again for these deeds. (Grandmothers of the
Plaza de Mayo in Carloto 1994: 32)

"What does your dance need? Your tango lacks scream.
Dance a tango that screams."

Afterword

This work addresses the diffuse nature of violence that makes it inextricable from other experiences. I have attempted to approach such pervasiveness through its everyday experience in Argentine life and its presence in the tango. I dwell, in order to avoid the sensationalization of violence, on its everyday particulars and its emergence in the routine practice of an art form rather than in major works. And I put emphasis on the continued experience and expression of violence in the aftermaths of terror, both in an aesthetic arena and in the lives of those who have not been protagonists of an episode or an era.

When violence explodes in an interaction with those we think we "know," or within our perceptions of beauty, it appears to be a contradiction. The experience of this contradiction escapes efforts to explain or analyze. It can be evoked, enacted, and communicated by the juxtaposition of heterogeneous fragments within a text with its own contradictions.

This text itself, then, is contradictory, performing the eruptions with which it deals.

Like violence, art is not communicated by "rational" discourses. The elements that I extract from my own life to use here are chosen and related to one another in a way that resonates in both Argentine culture—specifically, with the tango—and among readers elsewhere. I have attempted through writing to reconstruct an interaction with a cultural category—here the experience of a work or genre of art—for readers outside Argentina. I insert that experience into the interpretation of the art of another people. The reconstruction has made sense for the readers of the work because it builds on an experience familiar to them in many ways, my own. It has had the effect of distancing the form from its Argentine creators and performers, giving them a new perspective on *their* world.

Over the thirty years of my experience with Argentina, Argentines have lived moments that have become ever darker. Other areas of my work have increasingly concerned violence: economic, domestic, discursive. This pushed me to consider modes other than the analytic to deal with what I encountered in Argentine worlds. At the same time, it led me to concentrate on the aftermath of violence and the stolen stories of victims (1994; 1998). In a world where the experience of violence permeates further and further, to write in a mode that performs lived contradictions has spoken to specific forms of violence in the lives and art of specific actors. It has also helped avoid the danger of a naturalization or essentialization of the experiences of terror that share an unspeakable dimension but that also differ deeply one from the other.

In the world described here, violences are exclusions. Terror is absolute exclusion, the absolute lack of recourse: to the forces of order, to the law, to the family, to wealth, to any social ties. Exclusions involve turning a human being into a thing. I, as female and foreign, was often rendered an exotic object: Parallels between this process and other exclusionary objectifications opened windows for me onto Argentine culture, and Argentine culture opened windows onto my own.

Such a text may help us discover the multiple terrors lived daily as exclusion: sometimes spectacular and often subtle—in order to better our perception and diagnosis of the phenomenon. We need to concentrate on the task of formulating sufficiently strong statements not about but from within the suffering entailed by the violent ruptures these techniques enact. Perhaps their greatest resonance may be found in an everyday world haunted with collusions and complicities.

Works Cited

Abuelas de la Plaza de Mayo. 1994. In Estela Barnes de Carloto, "Removiendo escombros."

Bruchstein, Luís. 1994. "Un muro contra el terror." *Página 12* (7-22-94): 3.

Calvino, Italo. 1974. *Invisible Cities*, 62. New York: Harcourt Brace Jovanovich.

Carloto, Estela Barnes de. 1994. "Removiendo escombros." *Página 12* (7-22-94): 32.

Collier, Simon. 1986. *The Life, Music, and Times of Carlos Gardel.* Pittsburgh: University of Pittsburgh Press.

Feinmann, Jose Pablo. 1994. "El himno del pueblo de Israel." *Página 12* (7-23-94): 32.

Fischerman, Diego. 1994. "Entre ellos y nosotros." *Página 12* (7-23-94): 10.

González, Pablo. 1994. "'Hay mucha impunidad.'" *Página 12* (7-24-94): 15.

Mayer, Ralph. 1969. *A Dictionary of Art Terms and Techniques.* New York: Crowell.

Myers, Bernard S., ed. 1969. *McGraw-Hill Dictionary of Art.* New York: McGraw-Hill.

Il Nuovo Dizionario Hazon Garzanti. 1990. Milan: Garzanti Editore.

Osborne, Harold, ed. 1970. *The Oxford Companion to Art.* Oxford: Clarendon.

Rodríguez Marín, Francisco. [1882] 1989. *Piropos.* Buenos Aires: Andrómeda.

Sábato, Ernesto. 1968. *Tango: Discusión y clave.* 3d. ed. Buenos Aires: Editorial Losada.

Savigliano, Marta. 1995. *Tango and the Political Economy of Passion.* Boulder: Westview.

Taussig, Michael. 1993. *Mimesis and Alterity: A Particular History of the Senses.* New York: Routledge.

Taylor, Julie. 1994. "Aides-memoires and Cultural Amnesia." In *Body Politics: Disease, Desire, and the Family,* edited by Michael Ryan and Avery Gordon. Boulder: Westview.

———. 1998. "Accessing Narrative: The Gaucho and Europe in Argentina." *Cultural Critique* (spring).

Villaveces Izquierdo, Santiago. 1997. "Art and Media-tion: Reflections on Violence and Representation." In *Late Editions: Cultural Studies for the End of the Century,* vol. 4: *Cultural Producers in Perilous States,* edited by George E. Marcus. Chicago: University of Chicago Press.

Film cited

Solanas, Fernando. *Tangos: The Exile of Gardel,* 1986.

Julie Taylor is Associate Professor in the Department of
Anthropology at Rice University. She is the author of *Eva
Perón: The Myths of a Woman.*

Library of Congress Cataloging-in-Publication Data
Taylor, Julie.
Paper tangos / by Julie Taylor.
p. cm.—(Public planet books)
ISBN 0-8223-2175-0 (alk. paper).—
ISBN 0-8223-2191-2 (pbk.: alk. paper)
1. Tango (Dance)—Argentina—Psychological aspects.
I. Title.   II. Series.
GV1796.T3T39   1998   793.3'3—dc21   97-31240 CIP